With 1300 simple daily-use Kolam designs

Apartment Kolam's

KOLAM: The timeless art of South India

VIDYA SELVAM

To my beloved family members,

This book is dedicated to each and every one of you who have touched my life in profound ways. Your love, unwavering support, and unbreakable bonds have shaped my journey and filled my days with immeasurable joy. Through laughter and tears, triumphs, and challenges, you have stood by my side, reminding me of the power of connection and the beauty of family. This book is a testament to our shared experiences, the memories we hold dear, and the strength we draw from one another. With deepest gratitude, I dedicate this book to my remarkable family members who have forever enriched my life.

With all my heart,
Vidya Selvam.

Table of Contents

Chapter 1: Introduction and History of Kolam

Introduction to Kolam:

Kolam, also known as Rangoli, is a traditional art form originating from South India. It is a decorative design made on the floor using rice flour, coloured powders, or flower petals. It is a form of geometric art that involves creating intricate and colourful designs on the floors of homes, temples, and other public spaces. Kolam is an integral part of South Indian culture and is believed to have originated thousands of years ago. The practice of making Kolam's has been passed down from generation to generation and is primarily practiced by women who wake up early in the morning to draw these designs in front of their homes. Kolam's are believed to have originated as a way of feeding ants and other small insects that crawl on the ground, and eventually evolved into a form of art. The practice of creating Kolam is not just an artistic expression but is also seen as a way of welcoming guests and bringing good luck and prosperity to the household.

Kolam designs come in different shapes and sizes, ranging from simple geometric patterns to more intricate and elaborate designs. The most common shapes used in Kolam are dots, lines, squares, and circles, which are combined in various ways to create unique and beautiful designs. The designs are often inspired by nature, such as flowers, leaves, and animals, and also incorporate traditional symbols and motifs. The art of creating Kolam requires patience, creativity, and a steady hand. It's usually created by dropping the coloured rice flour or chalk powder onto the ground using the fingers. The process of creating Kolam can take anywhere from a few minutes to several hours, depending on the complexity of the design. In recent years, Kolam has gained wider recognition and appreciation as an art form, with people all over the world taking up the practice as a way of expressing their creativity and connecting with the rich cultural heritage of South India.

Origins of Kolam

The origins of Kolam are shrouded in mystery and have been the subject of much debate among scholars. However, it is believed that Kolam originated in the southern state of Tamil Nadu in India and has been practiced for thousands of years.

5 – 1	3 – 3	5 - 3	5 - 3
7 – 3	7 - 1	6 - 6	
7 – 1	5 - 5	7 - 3	

Some scholars believe that the practice of creating Kolam may have originated as a way of providing food for ants and other insects. The rice flour used in Kolam was believed to have antiseptic properties that kept insects at bay. The practice of creating Kolam was thus seen as a way of promoting the coexistence of humans and insects, which was an important aspect of ancient Tamil culture. Another theory suggests that Kolam has its roots in ancient spiritual practices. According to this theory, Kolam was used as a way of connecting with the divine and inviting good luck and prosperity into the home. It was believed that the intricate designs and patterns created using Kolam had symbolic meaning and were a way of communicating with the gods.

Whatever its origins may be, Kolam has played a vital role in the cultural and social fabric of South India for centuries. The practice of creating Kolam has evolved over time, with new materials and techniques being developed, and the designs becoming more elaborate and intricate. Today, Kolam is still a popular art form that is practiced in homes, temples, and public spaces throughout South India and beyond.

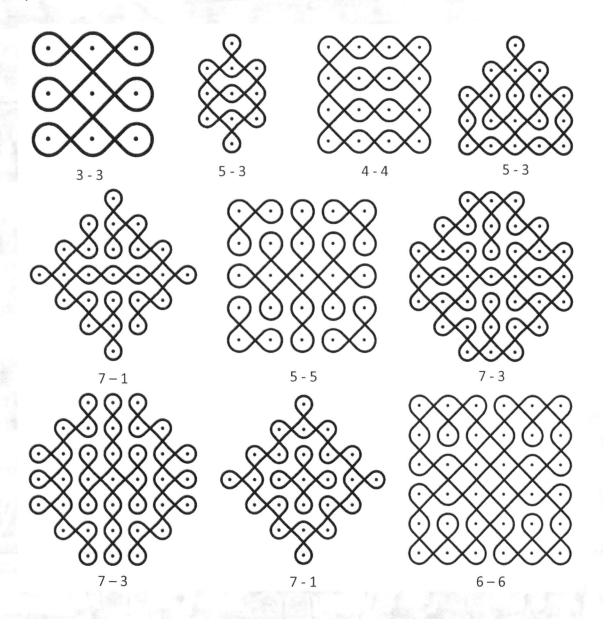

3 - 3   5 - 3   4 - 4   5 - 3

7 – 1   5 - 5   7 - 3

7 – 3   7 - 1   6 – 6

The Historical Roots of Kolam

The art of Kolam, has deep historical roots that can be traced back to ancient times. Kolam is a traditional form of art that is practiced in South India, particularly in the states of Tamil Nadu, Karnataka, and Andhra Pradesh. The practice of creating Kolam is believed to have originated thousands of years ago, during the ancient Tamil civilization, which flourished in South India between 200 BCE and 300 CE. Some scholars believe that the practice of creating Kolam dates back to the Indus Valley Civilization, which existed in the Indian subcontinent between 2600 BCE and 1900 BCE.

The earliest references to Kolam can be found in ancient Tamil literature, including the Sangam literature, which contains several references to Kolam, which was an integral part of daily life during that period. Some of the references to Kolam in Sangam literature include:

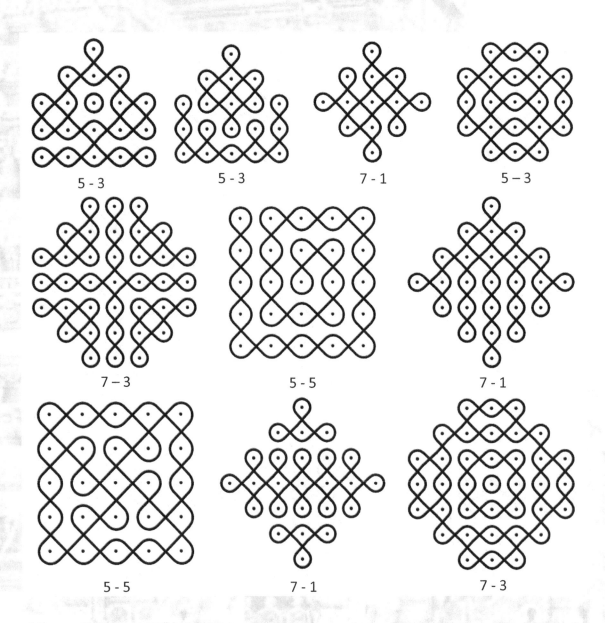

1. In the poem "**Nattrinai**," the author describes a scene where women are creating Kolam designs using rice flour and decorating their homes with flowers and other natural materials.
2. The poem "**Purananuru**" contains a reference to a woman who creates a beautiful Kolam design using colored sand and flowers to welcome her lover.
3. In the poem "**Kurunthokai**," the author describes a scene where a woman is creating a Kolam design using white rice flour, and the design is so intricate that it looks like a forest.
4. The poem "**Agananuru**" contains a reference to a group of women who are creating Kolam designs in a temple courtyard as part of a religious ceremony.
5. In the poem "**Patthupattu**," the author describes a scene where a woman is creating a Kolam design in front of her home to welcome her husband, who is returning from a long journey.

These references to Kolam in Sangam literature suggest that the practice of creating Kolam was an important part of daily life and had both social and religious significance. The designs created using Kolam were simple and geometric in the early period, but over time, they became more elaborate and intricate, incorporating traditional symbols and motifs, and drawing inspiration from nature.

5 - 3   3 – 3   5 - 3   4 - 4

5 - 5   7 - 1   7 - 3

7 – 1   7 - 3   6 - 6

History of Kolam

Kolam has been practiced in various forms and styles throughout South India for centuries. The earliest recorded evidence of the practice of Kolam can be found in ancient Tamil literature, which dates back to the Sangam period, between 300 BCE and 300 CE. The literature describes the practice of creating Kolam using rice flour and other natural materials as a form of decoration for special occasions and festivals.

During the Chola dynasty, which ruled South India from the 9th to the 13th century CE, Kolam became an integral part of daily life. The practice of creating Kolam was not just limited to special occasions but was also done every day as a way of welcoming guests and bringing good luck and prosperity to the household. The art of creating Kolam continued to evolve over the years and reached its pinnacle during the Nayak dynasty, which ruled South India from the 16th to the 18th century CE. During this period, Kolam became more elaborate and intricate, with designs inspired by nature and traditional symbols and motifs.

| 5 - 1 | 4 - 4 | 5 – 3 | 5 - 3 |

| 7 - 1 | 5 - 5 | 7 - 3 |

| 7 - 3 | 7 - 1 | 5 - 5 |

With the arrival of the British in India in the 18th century, the practice of creating Kolam began to decline. The British considered it to be a primitive and uncivilized practice, and as a result, it lost its popularity among the educated classes.

However, with the rise of the Indian independence movement in the early 20th century, there was a renewed interest in traditional Indian art forms, including Kolam. Artists and scholars began to study and revive the practice of creating Kolam, and it once again became a popular form of art and decoration.

Today, Kolam has not only survived the test of time but has also evolved and gained popularity around the world. It is now recognized as a form of art and is even taught in schools and colleges.

5 - 3   3 - 3   5 - 3   5 - 1

7 - 1   6 - 6   7 - 3

5 - 5   7 - 3   7 - 1

Chapter 2: Symbolism and Significance of Kolam

Symbolism in Kolam

Kolam, the traditional art form of South India, is not just a decorative practice but also holds deep symbolic meaning. The designs created using Kolam are often inspired by nature and are filled with symbolism that reflects the values, beliefs, and aspirations of the community.

Circle: The circle is a common shape in Kolam designs and is believed to represent unity, wholeness, and infinity. The circle is also associated with the concept of the cycle of life, death, and rebirth. Kolams with circular designs are often drawn during special occasions such as weddings and other auspicious events.

Dot: The dot is another common element in Kolam designs and is believed to represent the beginning of life. The dot is also associated with the concept of the bindu, which is the center point of creation. Kolams with dots are often drawn in a grid pattern, with the dots forming the basis of the design.

Lines and curves: Lines and curves are essential elements of Kolam designs and are believed to represent the flow of energy and movement. The lines and curves in Kolams are often drawn in a symmetrical pattern and are intended to create a sense of balance and harmony.

Flowers: Flowers are a common motif in Kolam designs and are believed to represent beauty, purity, and grace. Different types of flowers are associated with different deities in Hinduism. For example, the lotus flower is associated with Lord Vishnu, while the jasmine flower is associated with Goddess Lakshmi.

Animals: Animals are also a common motif in Kolam designs and are believed to represent different qualities and characteristics. For example, the peacock is associated with Lord Murugan and

is believed to represent beauty and grace. The elephant is associated with Lord Ganesha and is believed to represent wisdom and strength.

Colors: Colors are an essential part of Kolam designs and are believed to have different energies and meanings. For example, White is the most used color in Kolam, and it is believed to symbolize purity, peace, and clarity of thought. Red is often used to represent energy, passion, and love, while yellow is associated with knowledge, wisdom, and prosperity. By using different colors in their Kolams, artists can create a specific mood or atmosphere that is aligned with their intention.

Symbolism and Significance of Kolam

Kolam is not only a decorative practice but also has deep symbolic and cultural significance.

Welcoming guests and warding off evil: One of the primary purposes of creating Kolam designs is to welcome guests into the home and to ward off evil spirits. The designs are often created at the entrance of the house, and the intricate patterns and bright colors are believed to be attractive to positive energies and repel negative ones.

| 5 - 1 | 5 - 3 | 5 - 3 | 5 - 3 |

| 5 - 5 | 7 - 1 | 7 - 3 |

| 7 - 1 | 7 - 3 | 5 - 5 |

Invoking blessings of the gods: Kolam designs are also believed to be a way of communicating with the gods and invoking their blessings. The designs often feature traditional symbols and motifs that are associated with various deities and creating them is believed to be a form of devotion and offering to the gods.

Fertility and prosperity: Many Kolam design feature symbols of fertility and prosperity, such as fish, lotus flowers, and mangoes. These symbols are believed to bring good luck and abundance into the home and are often created during festivals and auspicious occasions.

Connection with nature: Kolam designs often draw inspiration from nature, featuring patterns and motifs that are reminiscent of flowers, leaves, and other natural elements. This is believed to create a connection with nature and to remind people of the beauty and harmony of the natural world.

Community and tradition: The practice of creating Kolam designs is often a communal one, with women coming together to create elaborate designs during festivals and other celebrations. This reinforces a sense of community and tradition and helps to preserve the cultural heritage of South India.

3 - 3   5 - 3   5 - 1   4 - 4

7 - 1   7 - 3   6 - 6

5 - 5   7 - 1   7 - 3

Spiritual significance: Kolam is often used in spiritual practices, and the kolam designs are believed to have spiritual significance. The symbols and motifs used in Kolam designs represent various aspects of the divine and are believed to invoke their blessings.

Cultural heritage: Kolam is an important part of the cultural heritage of South India and is often passed down from generation to generation. The practice of creating kolam designs is a way of connecting, with one's cultural roots and preserving traditional art forms.

Social significance: Kolam is often used as a way of bringing communities together. During festivals and special occasions, people come together to create elaborate Kolam designs and celebrate their cultural heritage.

Kolam is an art form that is deeply rooted in the cultural and spiritual heritage of South India. It has both symbolic and practical significance and continues to be an important part of daily life and social practices in the region.

Cultural Significance

Kolam is a vibrant and colorful form of art that holds immense cultural significance in the region. Here are some of the cultural significances of Kolam:

Preservation of tradition: Kolam is a practice that has been passed down through generations and is an important part of South Indian culture. The intricate designs and traditional motifs used in Kolam reflect the rich cultural heritage of the region, and the practice of creating Kolam designs helps to preserve this tradition and pass it on to future generations.

Expression of creativity: Kolam is a highly creative art form, and the intricate designs created reflect the creativity and artistic expression of the people who create them. This practice provides a platform for artistic expression, allowing people to explore different colors, patterns, and designs while also preserving their cultural heritage.

Celebration of nature: Many Kolam designs draw inspiration from nature, featuring patterns and motifs that are reminiscent of flowers, leaves, and other natural elements. This practice celebrates

5 - 1   5 - 3   4 - 4   5 - 3

7 - 1   5 - 5   7 - 3

7 - 3   7 - 1   6 - 6

the beauty and harmony of the natural world and helps to create a connection between people and the environment.

Fostering community spirit: Kolam is often a communal practice, with women coming together to create intricate designs during festivals and other occasions. This reinforces a sense of community and togetherness and helps to promote social cohesion.

Celebrating auspicious occasions: Kolam is an integral part of auspicious occasions such as weddings, religious festivals, and other important events. The designs created during these occasions are often elaborate and feature traditional symbols and motifs that are associated with the festival or occasion. This reinforces a sense of community and tradition and helps to keep the culture alive.

Connection with spirituality: Kolam is not just a decorative art form, but it also has deep spiritual significance. The practice of creating Kolam designs is believed to be a form of devotion and offering to the gods. The designs often feature traditional symbols and motifs that are associated with various deities and creating them is believed to invoke the blessings of the gods.

Spiritual Significance of Kolam

Beyond its aesthetic value, Kolam holds great spiritual significance. Kolams are often created outside homes, temples, and other sacred spaces, and are believed to invite positive energy and ward off negative forces. Kolams are also believed to bring good luck, prosperity, and harmony to the household.

In Hinduism, the act of drawing a Kolam is considered a way to invite the goddess of wealth and prosperity, Lakshmi, into the home. It is believed that the intricate designs and the colors used in the Kolam have a positive impact on the mind and soul, and the act of drawing it is considered a form of meditation.

One of the most significant aspects of Kolam is its use of geometry and symmetry. The intricate patterns and designs are often based on sacred geometries, such as the Sri Yantra, and are believed to help align the energy of the space with the cosmos.

5 - 1   5 - 3   4 - 4   5 - 3

7 - 1   7 - 3   5 - 5

5 - 5   7 - 1   7 - 3

The use of symmetry is also significant, as it represents balance and harmony, which are important spiritual principles.

Kolam is also considered to be a form of offering to the gods. The rice flour used in the Kolam is believed to be food for ants and other small insects and drawing Kolam is seen as an act of kindness towards these creatures. It is also believed that drawing Kolam is a way of offering gratitude to Mother Earth for her bounty and blessings.

The traditional designs of Kolam are inspired by nature, and many of them have deep symbolic meaning. For example, the lotus flower is a common motif in Kolam designs and is believed to represent purity and enlightenment. Similarly, the peacock, which is often depicted in Kolams, is considered a sacred bird in Hinduism, and is associated with Lord Murugan. This connection to nature is significant because it helps us to connect with the larger web of life, and to recognize our place in the natural order of things.

Kolams are not just limited to Hinduism. They are also an important part of other Indian religions like Jainism and Buddhism. In Jainism, the practice of drawing Kolams is considered a way to cultivate

mindfulness and non-violence. In Buddhism, Kolams are used as a form of meditation and are drawn to represent the impermanence of life and the interconnectedness of all things.

The Symbolism of Different Kolam Designs

The intricate patterns and designs of Kolams are not just for decoration but also carry symbolic meanings that reflect the beliefs and values of the community. Here are some of the common Kolam designs and their symbolic significance.

Geometric Kolam: Geometric Kolam designs often feature squares, circles, and triangles and are believed to represent the balance and harmony of the universe. These designs are often used to promote inner peace and spiritual growth.

Conch Shell Kolam: The conch shell is a symbol of power and purity. It is used in Hindu rituals and is believed to produce the primordial sound "Om," which is the sound of the universe. The conch shell is also associated with Lord Vishnu.

Paisley Kolam: The paisley is a popular motif in Kolam designs and is believed to represent fertility and abundance. It is also associated with the goddess Lakshmi.

Peacock Feather Kolam: Peacock feathers are a symbol of beauty and spirituality. The intricate patterns and colors of the peacock feather represent the beauty and diversity of life. Peacock Feather Kolams is often drawn to celebrate festivals and weddings.

Mango Leaf Kolam: The mango leaf is a symbol of prosperity and fertility. It is often drawn during the harvest season to signify the abundance of nature. The design of Mango Leaf Kolams is simple yet elegant, representing simplicity and beauty of life.

Mango Kolam: The mango is a symbol of good fortune in Indian culture. Mango Kolams is believed to bring abundance and prosperity to the household. The mango is also associated with the Hindu god Lord Ganesha, who is often depicted holding a mango in his hand.

Sun Kolam: Sun is an important symbol in Hinduism and is associated with many deities, including Lord Surya and Lord Vishnu. The Sun is believed to represent life, energy, and vitality. Sun

5 - 1   5 – 3   5 - 3   5 - 3

7 - 1   7 - 3   5 - 5

5 - 5   7 - 1   7 - 3

Kolams are also believed to bring good health and happiness to the household.

Peacock Kolam: The peacock is a sacred bird in Hinduism, and it is often depicted in Kolam designs. Peacock Kolams is believed to bring good luck and prosperity to the household. The peacock's beautiful feathers are said to represent purity, grace, and elegance. Peacock Kolams is also associated with Lord Murugan, who is often depicted riding a peacock.

Lotus Kolam: The lotus flower is a common motif in Kolam designs and is believed to symbolize purity, enlightenment, and rebirth. The lotus is a symbol of spiritual awakening and is associated with many Hindu deities, including Lord Vishnu and Goddess Lakshmi. The lotus is also believed to represent the path to enlightenment and the overcoming of obstacles.

Swastika Kolam: Swastika is an ancient symbol that has been used for thousands of years in Hinduism, Buddhism, and Jainism. The Swastika is believed to represent good luck, prosperity, and well-being. The four arms of the Swastika are said to represent the four Vedas, the ancient Hindu scriptures. Swastika Kolams is often drawn on special occasions such as weddings and other auspicious events.

5 – 1   5 - 3   4 – 4   5 - 3

7 – 1   7 – 3   6 - 6

5 – 5   7 – 1   7 - 3

Chapter 3: Materials and Techniques

Materials Used for Making Kolam

Each material has its unique properties and characteristics, and the choice of material depends on the artist's preference, the occasion, and the availability of materials.

Rice Flour: Rice flour is the most commonly used material for making Kolam. It is made by grinding rice into a fine powder and is used to create intricate designs on the floor. Rice flour is preferred because it is easily available and has a smooth texture. It is also mixed with water to form a paste, which is then used to create the design on the floor.

Colored Powders: Colored powders are also commonly used for making Kolam. They are available in a wide range of colors, and the designs created using colored powders are often bright and vibrant. Colored powders are particularly popular during festivals such as Diwali, when people decorate their homes with colorful Kolams.

| 5 - 1 | 5 - 3 | 5 - 3 | 5 - 3 |

| 7 - 1 | 5 - 5 | 7 - 3 |

| 7 - 1 | 5 - 5 | 7 - 3 |

Chalk Powder: Chalk powder is another common material used for making Kolam. It is available in a variety of colors, and the colors can be mixed to create new shades. Chalk powder is usually used for special occasions and festivals, and the designs created using chalk powder are often vibrant and colorful.

Flowers and Petals: Flowers and petals are sometimes used for making Kolam. They are particularly popular during festivals such as Pongal and Onam. The designs created using flowers and petals are often colorful and fragrant, and they add a touch of beauty and elegance to the Kolam.

Sand: Sand is another material that is sometimes used for making Kolam. Sand Kolams are particularly popular in coastal regions of South India, where sand is abundant. Sand Kolams are usually created using colored sand, and the designs are often simple and geometric.

Turmeric Powder: Turmeric powder is a traditional material used for making Kolam. It is considered to be auspicious and is believed to have antimicrobial properties. Turmeric Kolams are usually created using a mixture of turmeric powder and water, and the designs are often simple and traditional.

5 - 1   5 - 3   4 - 4   5 - 3

5 - 5   7 - 1   7 – 3

7 - 1   7 - 3   6 - 6

Cow Dung: Cow dung is also sometimes used for making Kolam as the base applied on the floor. It is believed to have purifying properties and is considered to be sacred in Hindu culture. Cow dung Kolams are usually created by mixing cow dung with water and applying it to the floor in a circular motion to create the kolam base.

Sawdust: Sawdust is a material that is sometimes used for making Kolam. It is often mixed with color to create unique designs. Sawdust Kolams are popular in some parts of Tamil Nadu and Kerala.

Stencil: Stencils are sometimes used for making Kolam. They are made of plastic or metal and are available in different shapes and sizes. The stencil is placed on the floor, and the design is created by filling in the stencil with rice flour or colored powders.

Use of Colors in Kolam

Colors play an essential role in the creation of Kolams. They add vibrancy and beauty to the designs and help to bring out the intricate patterns and details. The use of colors in Kolams is not just

5 - 3   5 - 3   5 - 1   5 - 3

7 - 1   7 - 3   5 - 5

5 - 5   7 - 1   7 - 3

for aesthetic purposes but also has symbolic meanings associated with them. The choice of colors often depends on the artist's creativity and imagination. In this chapter, we will explore the use of colors in Kolams.

White: White is the most commonly used color in Kolams. The white color represents purity, simplicity, and tranquility. White Kolams are often created using rice flour or chalk powder and are typically created in simple geometric shapes and are perfect for daily use.

Red: Red is a vibrant color that is often used in Kolam to symbolize power, passion, and strength. It also represents love, marriage, and fertility. Red is usually used in combination with other colors, and it is obtained from natural sources such as red sand and vermillion powder. It is often used during weddings and other auspicious occasions.

Yellow: Yellow is a bright and cheerful color that is often used in Kolam to symbolize happiness, prosperity, and wealth. It also represents the sun, which is considered as a symbol of life, energy, and vitality. Yellow is obtained from turmeric powder, and it is used to create intricate designs that add vibrancy and elegance to the Kolam. It is often used during festivals such as Pongal and Onam.

3 - 3	5 - 3	5 - 1	5 - 3
5 - 5	7 – 1	7 - 3
7 - 1	7 – 3	6 - 6

Green: Green is a soothing color that is often used in Kolam to symbolize nature, growth, and harmony. It also represents fertility, health, and prosperity. Green is obtained from natural sources such as leaves, grass, and green powders, and it is used to create intricate designs that add a touch of nature to the Kolam. It is often used during the spring season and during festivals such as Navratri.

Blue: Blue is a calming and peaceful color that is often used in Kolam to symbolize the sky and the sea. It represents serenity, wisdom, and spirituality. Blue is obtained from natural sources such as blue sand and blue powders, and it is used to create intricate designs that add a touch of tranquility to the Kolam. Blue Kolams are particularly popular during festivals such as Diwali.

Purple: Purple is a color associated with luxury, royalty, and creativity. Purple Kolams are created using a combination of red and blue colored powders, and they are perfect for creating intricate designs.

Orange: Orange is a vibrant and energetic color that is often used in Kolam to symbolize enthusiasm, creativity, and joy. It also represents the sun, which is considered as a symbol of life, and vitality. Orange is obtained from natural sources such as orange powders and marigold flowers,

| 5 - 1 | 5 - 3 | 5 - 3 | 5 - 3 |

| 7 - 1 | 7 - 3 | 5 - 5 |

| 5 - 5 | 7 - 1 | 7 - 3 |

and it is used to create intricate designs that add a touch of liveliness to the Kolam. It is often used during festivals such as Holi and Diwali.

Pink: Pink is a color associated with love, compassion, kindness, and affection. Pink Kolams are created using a combination of red and white colored powders, and they are perfect for creating designs with floral motifs. It is often used during weddings and other romantic occasions.

The Techniques of Kolam

There are several techniques used to create Kolam designs, each with its own unique characteristics and styles.

Freehand Technique: The freehand technique is the most common and widely used technique in Kolam. This technique involves creating the design by hand, without the use of any tools or stencils. The artist begins by drawing the outline of the design using a single continuous line. The rest of the design is filled in by creating smaller lines and shapes within the outline. The This technique requires a steady hand and a lot of practice to master.

Dotted Technique: The dotted technique involves creating the design by placing dots on the ground in a specific pattern and connecting them to create the design. This technique is often used for more complex designs that require precise placement of elements.

Pulli Kolam Technique: The Pulli Kolam is a variation of the dotted technique which involves creating a series of dots in a specific pattern and connecting them to form the design. It is often used for designs that require intricate patterns and repetition. Pulli Kolam is a popular technique among the people of Tamil Nadu.

Grid Technique: The grid technique involves dividing the ground into a grid of squares or rectangles. The artist then creates the design by filling in the squares with different shapes and lines. This technique is often used for designs that require symmetry and balance.

Freehand with Grid Technique: The Freehand with Grid technique is a combination of the freehand and grid techniques. The artist creates the design by drawing a rough outline freehand and then uses a grid to fill in the details. This technique is often used for designs that require a balance between freehand elements and precise details.

Powdered Color Technique: The powdered color technique involves using colored powders to create the design. The artist mixes the desired colors with rice flour or chalk powder and applies them to the ground using fingers or a piece of cloth. This technique is commonly used to create vibrant and bold designs.

Wet Rice Flour Technique: The wet rice flour technique involves mixing rice flour with water to create a paste-like consistency. The artist then applies the paste to the ground and creates the design. This technique is often used to create subtle and delicate designs that are meant to blend in with their surroundings.

Flower Petal Technique: The flower petal technique involves using flower petals to create the design. Artist places the petals on the ground in specific pattern and connects them to form the design. This technique is often used for designs that require natural elements and a sense of organic beauty.

Sandy Color Technique: The sandy color technique involves using colored sand to create the design. The artist applies the sand to the ground using fingers or a piece of cloth and creates the design. This technique is often used to create intricate designs with precise details.

5 - 1   5 - 3   4 - 4   5 - 3

7 - 1   7 - 3   6 - 6

5 - 5   7 - 1   7 - 3

Designing a Kolam

Designing a Kolam is a beautiful and intricate process that involves creating unique patterns and shapes. Designing a Kolam requires patience, creativity, and a deep understanding of the art form's cultural significance. To create a Kolam, one must have a basic understanding of the different techniques and styles used in this art form. Here are some steps to design a Kolam:

Step 1: Choose a Design

The first step in designing a Kolam is to choose a design. The design can be traditional or modern. There are several traditional Kolam designs to choose from, such as flower designs, geometric patterns, and deity designs. Alternatively, you can create your unique design or modify an existing design to suit your preferences. You can find inspiration for your design from books, websites, or by observing other Kolam artists.

Step 2: Select a Spot

Once you have chosen your design, select a suitable spot to create your Kolam. The spot should be a flat surface, such as a concrete floor, and should be clean and dry.

Step 3: Select Colors

Once you have chosen your design, select the colors you want to use. The colors used in Kolam are usually natural and organic, such as rice flour or chalk powder. The colors you choose can have symbolic meanings and bring life to the design.

Step 4: Prepare the Surface

Before starting to draw the design, clean the surface thoroughly to remove any dirt, debris, or stains.

Step 5: Create the Outline

Start creating the Kolam design by following the chosen technique. You can use freehand,

dotted, grid, or Pulli Kolam techniques, depending on the complexity and style of your design. Remember to be patient and take your time to create each element of the design. Start by drawing the main lines and shapes of the design using the freehand technique. Use the dotted technique to create more intricate patterns and details.

Step 6: Add Details

Once the outline is complete, you can add more details to the design using different techniques. You can use the grid technique to create symmetrical designs or the Pulli Kolam technique to create repetitive patterns.

Step 7: Fill in the Design.

After creating the outline and adding details, start filling in the design with colors. You can use different colors to add depth and dimension to the design. Use natural colors like rice flour, turmeric powder, and vermilion to create a traditional look.

Step 8: Finishing Touches

Once you have completed the design, add finishing touches to the Kolam. You can add small details or highlights to make the design stand out. You can also add flowers or other decorations around the Kolam to enhance its beauty.

Step 9: Clean Up the Design

Once the design is complete, the final step is to clean up the design. Use a soft brush to remove any excess rice flour or chalk powder from the design. This will help to ensure that the design looks clean and crisp.

Step 10: Enjoy and Share

The final step is to enjoy and share your Kolam design with others.

Traditional Designs Used in Kolam

Traditional designs used in Kolam often have symbolic meanings and are created for auspicious

5 - 1	5 - 3	4 - 4	5 - 3
7 - 1	7 - 3	6 - 6
5 - 5	7 - 1	7 - 3

occasions such as weddings, festivals, and other celebrations. Here are some of the most common traditional designs used in Kolam:

Peacock Kolam: Peacock Kolam is a popular traditional design used in Kolam. The design features a beautiful peacock with its feathers spread out in vibrant colors. This design often includes intricate patterns and flowing lines. The peacock symbolizes beauty, grace, and pride.

Hridaya Kamalam: Hridaya Kamalam is a traditional design that consists of a lotus flower with multiple layers of petals. This design is believed to represent the heart chakra and is often used for meditation and spiritual practices.

Swastika Kolam: The Swastika Kolam is a common traditional design used in Kolam. The design features the Swastika symbol, which is considered a symbol of prosperity and good luck in Indian culture.

Kalyana Kolam: Kalyana Kolam is a traditional design that is often created for weddings and other auspicious occasions. This design consists of intricate patterns and motifs that represent fertility, prosperity, and good luck.

5 - 3   5 - 3   5 - 1   5 - 3

7 - 1   7 - 3   5 - 5

7 - 3   5 - 5   7 - 1

Pongal Kolam: Pongal Kolam is a traditional design that is created during the Pongal festival, which celebrates the harvest season. This design consists of various natural elements such as flowers, fruits, and animals that represent abundance and prosperity.

Neli Kolam: Neli Kolam is a traditional design that consists of intertwined lines and loops. This design is believed to represent the unity and interconnectedness of all living beings.

Geometric Kolam: Geometric Kolam designs are created using precise shapes and patterns. These designs often involve intricate interlocking shapes and lines that create a beautiful and complex design.

Radial Kolam: Radial Kolam is a design that features radial symmetry, where the design is mirrored around a central point. This design often includes intricate patterns and geometric shapes.

Floral Kolam: Floral Kolam designs feature different types of beautiful flowers and leaves arranged in a pattern. These designs often use bright colors and intricate details to create a stunning design.

5 - 1 5 - 3 4 - 4 5 - 3

7 - 1 7 - 3 6 - 6

5 - 5 7 - 1 7 - 3

Animal Kolam: Animal Kolam designs feature different animals, such as elephants, horses, and birds. These designs often use bold colors and intricate details to create a visually stunning and meaningful design.

Lamp Kolam: Lamp Kolam designs feature lamps arranged in a pattern. The lamps symbolize light, wisdom, and knowledge and are often created for festivals such as Diwali.

Contemporary Designs in Kolam

Contemporary designs in kolam are characterized by their use of bold, geometric patterns and vibrant colors. Unlike traditional designs, which often feature natural elements like flowers or animals, contemporary kolams are more abstract and often draw inspiration from modern art and design. Contemporary kolam artists are also experimenting with new materials and techniques, such as using colored sand or even LED lights to create their designs.

Geometric Patterns: Contemporary kolam designs are often characterized by bold, geometric patterns that are visually striking. These designs often feature intricate shapes, lines, and angles that create a sense of movement and depth.

Mandala Designs: Mandala designs are circular patterns that often feature a central point surrounded by intricate geometric shapes and lines. These designs are popular in contemporary kolam art and can be quite large in size, spanning the entire front of a home or temple.

Pixel Art: Pixel art is a design style that originated in video games and computer graphics. Contemporary kolam artists have adapted this style to create intricate and detailed designs using small dots of colored powders arranged in a grid-like formation.

3D Kolams: Using new techniques and materials, contemporary kolam artists are creating stunning 3D designs that appear to pop out of the ground. These designs often use a combination of colored powders and materials like sand, stones, and flowers to create depth and texture.

Social and Environmental Themes: Some contemporary kolam artists are incorporating social and environmental themes into their designs. These designs often feature messages of peace, love, and unity, as well as symbols of environmentalism and sustainability.

Pop Culture References: Contemporary kolam artists are also incorporating pop culture references into their designs. These designs often feature characters from movies, TV shows, and video games, as well as famous musicians and other pop culture icons.

The Importance of Symmetry in Kolam

Symmetry is an important aspect of kolam. The use of symmetry in kolam is significant for several reasons, including its cultural and religious significance, and its aesthetic appeal. One of the primary reasons why symmetry is crucial is that it helps to create a sense of balance and harmony in kolam designs.

In many kolam designs, symmetry is achieved by creating a mirror image of the design along a central axis, using repeating patterns and motifs. This creates a sense of order and balance in the design, which is aesthetically pleasing to the eye. Symmetry in kolam also holds symbolic significance. In Hinduism, symmetry represents order, balance, and harmony in the universe. The creation of a symmetrical kolam design is seen as a way to connect with these higher spiritual principles.

Additionally, symmetry creates a visual balance that is pleasing to the eye. The repetition of patterns and motifs creates a sense of continuity and cohesion, making the design feel complete and harmonious. This is especially important in large kolams, which can span several feet in length and width.

| 5 - 1 | 5 - 3 | 5 - 3 | 5 - 3 |

| 7 - 1 | 7 - 3 | 5 - 5 |

| 5 - 5 | 7 - 1 | 7 - 3 |

Furthermore, the use of symmetry in kolam allows for a high degree of precision and accuracy in the design. Kolam artists use a variety of tools and techniques to ensure that their designs are perfectly symmetrical, from measuring and marking out the design to using stencils and templates. Creating a symmetrical design requires a high level of skill and attention to detail, which is why kolam artists often spend hours creating these intricate designs.

The Importance of Geometry in Kolam

Geometry plays a crucial role in kolam, a traditional art form that has been practiced in South India for centuries. Geometry is an essential aspect of kolam, and its importance can be seen in several ways.

Firstly, geometry is important in kolam because it provides the underlying structure for the designs. Kolam designs are typically created using a grid-like structure, with various shapes and patterns arranged within the grid. The use of geometry in this way helps to create a sense of order and balance

in the designs and allows the artist to create complex and intricate patterns that would not be possible without a structured approach.

Secondly, geometry is important in kolam because it allows for the creation of complex and intricate designs. Kolam artists often use intricate geometric shapes, such as triangles, circles, and hexagons, to create their designs. These shapes can be combined and arranged in a variety of ways to create unique and beautiful designs that are both visually striking and intellectually stimulating.

Thirdly, geometry is important in kolam because it requires a high level of skill and expertise to create. Creating intricate geometric designs in kolam requires a great deal of precision and attention to detail, as well as an understanding of mathematical concepts such as symmetry and tessellation. In this way, kolam can be seen as a form of intellectual and artistic expression that requires both creativity and technical skill.

42

Chapter 4: Types and Styles of Kolam

Different Types of Kolam

Over time, different types of kolam have emerged, each with its own unique style and characteristics. Here are some of the most popular types of kolam:

Pulli Kolam: Pulli kolam is the most basic type of kolam and involves creating designs using dots. The dots are placed in a specific pattern, and the design is created by joining the dots using lines and curves. Pulli kolams are often created by beginners and are simple in design.

Padi Kolam: Padi Kolam is a type of kolam that is created using parallel lines. The design is created by drawing a series of parallel lines and then connecting them together in a specific pattern. Padi Kolam is known for its simple yet elegant designs.

5 - 1   5 - 3   4 - 4   5 - 3

7 - 1   7 - 3   6 - 6

5 - 5   7 - 1   7 - 3

Sikku Kolam: Sikku kolam, also known as chikku kolam, is a type of kolam that features intricate, interlocking designs. It involves creating a series of lines and curves that loop around each other to create visually stunning patten.

Kambi Kolam: Kambi kolam, also known as curved line kolam, is a type of kolam that features flowing, curved lines. The artist creates a series of curves that interlock and overlap to create a visually stunning and intricate pattern.

Kavi Kolam: Kavi kolam is a type of kolam that involves creating designs using rice flour paste. The paste is used to draw intricate patterns and designs directly onto the ground. Kavi kolams are often created for special occasions and are considered to be a form of ritual art.

Freehand Kolam: Freehand kolam involves creating designs without the use of dots. This type of kolam is more challenging than pulli kolam and requires a higher level of skill and creativity. Freehand kolams are often created by experienced kolam artists and can be quite intricate and detailed.

Rangoli: Rangoli is a type of kolam that is created using colored powders or flower petals. Rangoli designs are often more vibrant and colorful than other types of kolam and can incorporate a wide range of shapes and patterns.

5 - 1   5 - 3   5 - 3   5 - 3

7 - 1   5 - 5   7 - 3

7 - 3   7 - 1   5 - 5

44

Pulli Kolam

Pulli Kolam, also known as dotted kolam, is a popular type of kolam that is practiced in South India. The word "pulli" means dot or point in Tamil, and this type of kolam involves creating a design using a grid of dots as a guide. The dots are typically arranged in a symmetrical pattern and serve as the foundation for the design. The word "pulli" means "dot" in Tamil, and pulli kolam is characterized by the use of small dots arranged in a specific pattern, depending on the design that the artist wishes to create. The artist connects the dots with lines and curves to create a beautiful and intricate design.

Pulli kolam designs can be simple or complex, depending on the number of dots used and the pattern created. The dots can be arranged in a variety of shapes, including diamonds, squares, rectangles, and triangles. The lines and curves that connect the dots can be straight, curved, or a combination of both. Pulli Kolam designs are typically symmetrical, which means that they are the same on both sides of the central axis. The symmetry is an important part of the design, as it creates a sense of balance and harmony.

| 5 - 1 | 5 - 3 | 4 - 4 | 5 - 3 |

| 7 - 1 | 7 - 3 | 6 - 6 |

| 5 - 5 | 7 - 1 | 7 - 3 |

The artist can also incorporate different colors and textures into the design, using colored powders, flowers, or even grains to create a unique and visually stunning work of art. In addition to its aesthetic appeal, pulli kolam is also considered to be a spiritual practice. It is believed to bring good luck and prosperity to the home, and it is often created as a daily ritual by women in South Indian households.

Sikku Kolam

Sikku Kolam, also known as Chikku Kolam or Neli Kolam, is a traditional art form from South India that is known for its intricate and complex designs. Unlike other types of kolam that use dots or grids as a guide, Sikku Kolam involves creating a series of interlocking lines and curves to form a visually stunning and intricate pattern. The word "sikku" or "chikku" means twisted or braided in Tamil, which refers to the way the lines and curves are twisted and braided together to create the design. The process of creating a Sikku Kolam is both time-consuming and labor-intensive, requiring a great deal of skill, patience, and attention to detail.

| 5 - 1 | 5 - 3 | 5 - 3 | 5 - 3 |

| 7 - 3 | 7 - 1 | 5 - 5 |

| 7 - 1 | 5 - 5 | 7 - 3 |

To create a Sikku Kolam, the artist starts by drawing a small central design, which is then surrounded by a series of concentric circles or squares. The artist then begins to create a series of interlocking lines and curves that connect the central design to the outer border. The lines and curves are drawn in a continuous motion, without lifting the hand or breaking the flow of the design. One of the unique features of Sikku Kolam is its use of interlocking designs. The patterns are created in such a way that they fit together like puzzle pieces, with each element of the design flowing seamlessly into the next. This creates a sense of continuity and fluidity that is visually striking and impressive.

Sikku kolam designs can vary in size and complexity, from simple and straightforward to highly intricate and detailed. The designs often incorporate traditional motifs such as flowers, birds, and geometric patterns, as well as cultural and religious symbols that hold significance in the community. Sikku Kolams are often created during special occasions and festivals, and they are an important part of South Indian culture. They are believed to bring good luck and prosperity to the home, and they are often created as a form of spiritual practice or meditation.

47

Padi Kolam

The term "padi" refers to the steps that are used to create the design, which consists of a series of parallel lines that are intersected by vertical and horizontal lines to create a grid-like pattern. The resulting design is often symmetrical and features intricate patterns and shapes.

To create a Padi Kolam, the artist starts by drawing a series of parallel lines that are spaced evenly apart. These lines act as a guide for the stepped patterns that are created by repeating a simple geometric shape or motif in a step-like manner. The size and spacing of the motifs can vary, creating different levels of complexity and visual interest in the design. The design is then repeated, with each layer offset from the previous layer, to create a three-dimensional effect. One of the unique features of Padi Kolam is its use of perspective. The layers of the design create a sense of depth and dimensionality that is visually striking and impressive. The use of perspective also creates a sense of movement and flow, with the eye being drawn from one layer of the design to the next.

Another unique feature of Padi Kolam is its use of symmetry. The design is created in such a way that it is perfectly balanced and harmonious. The use of symmetry creates a sense of order and stability, which is believed to bring good luck and prosperity to the home. Padi Kolams are often created during special occasions and festivals. In addition to its cultural significance, Padi Kolam is also appreciated for its artistic value. The intricate and complex designs require a great deal of skill and patience to create, and they are a true test of an artist's ability. The practice of creating Padi Kolams has been passed down through generations, and it continues to be an important part of South Indian art and culture today.

Kambi Kolam

The origins of Kambi Kolam can be traced back to ancient Tamil Nadu, where it was believed to have been used as a form of prayer and meditation. The term "Kambi Kolam" is derived from the Tamil words "Kambi" which means wire like or curved lines. Thus, Kambi Kolam is a form of art that involves creating intricate designs using curved lines. It is the hybrid of Sikku and Padi Kolam.

Kambi Kolam is an intricate art form that involves drawing a series of small steps that interconnect to create a larger pattern. These steps are usually drawn in a grid-like pattern and can range from simple to highly complex designs. Some Kambi Kolams are made up of straight lines and simple geometric shapes, while others incorporate intricate curves and curves with loops.

Creating a Kambi Kolam is a time-consuming process, the intricate and detailed designs require a great deal of patience, skill, and practice to master, and many artists spend years perfecting their craft. It is often passed down from generation to generation, with mothers and grandmothers teaching their daughters and granddaughters how to create these beautiful designs.

In addition to being a form of decoration, Kambi Kolam also has cultural and spiritual significance. It is believed to bring good luck and positive energy to the home and the people living in it. It is also a way of offering prayers and expressing gratitude to the gods and goddesses.

5 - 1   5 - 3   5 - 3   5 - 3

7 - 1   5 - 5   7 - 3

7 - 3   7 - 1   5 - 5

Margazhi Kolam

The practice of drawing Margazhi Kolam is believed to have started as a way to welcome the Hindu goddess Andal during the month of Margazhi, which falls between mid-December and mid-January. Margazhi is considered to be a sacred month in the Hindu calendar and is believed to be an auspicious time for spiritual practices. Some Scholars point out, the practice of creating Margazhi Kolam is believed to have originated from the need to provide food for ants and other small insects during the cold months of Margazhi.

Margazhi Kolam designs are often inspired by nature and typically feature geometric shapes, floral patterns, symbols of deities and auspicious symbols such as the lotus, peacock, and elephant. The designs are usually created using a dot grid, and the patterns are drawn by joining the dots using curved and straight lines. The designs are often complex and require a great deal of skill and patience to create. The kolams can range in size from small designs that fit in the palm of the hand to large designs that cover the entire floor of the entrance. Some of the more elaborate designs can take several hours to complete.

One of the unique features of Margazhi Kolam is that the designs are not static and are often modified and embellished on a daily basis. This allows the Kolams to evolve over time and reflect the creativity and artistic vision of the creator. The Kolams are also believed to have a spiritual significance and are often created as a form of meditation and worship.

In recent years, Margazhi Kolam has gained popularity beyond its traditional boundaries and is now recognized as a unique art form that represents the cultural heritage of Tamil Nadu. There are now Kolam competitions held throughout the state, and the art form has been showcased at international exhibitions.

Rangoli Kolam

Rangoli Kolam is a decorative design created on the floor using colorful powders, flowers, or grains. Rangoli is a Sanskrit word that means "colorful design" or "pattern". Rangoli Kolam is a popular form of art throughout India and is known by different names in different regions. For example, it is called Alpana in West Bengal, Aripana in Bihar, and Mandana in Rajasthan.

5 - 1   5 - 3   5 - 3   5 - 3

7 - 1   7 - 3   5 - 5

5 - 5   7 - 1   7 - 3

Rangoli Kolam is an important part of many Indian festivals and celebrations, such as Diwali, Navratri, and Pongal. The designs are often inspired by nature, and include images of flowers, birds, animals, and geometric shapes. The process of creating a Rangoli Kolam begins with cleaning the ground and sprinkling it with water to make it moist. Then, the artist uses her fingers to draw a series of dots in a specific pattern, which serves as the basis for the design. From there, she connects the dots using lines and curves to create the final design. The colors used in the designs are typically bright and vibrant and are chosen to complement the surrounding environment.

Rangoli Kolam is not only a form of art, but also a way of fostering a sense of community and social interaction. Women often gather in groups to create the kolams, and the practice serves as a way for them to connect with one another and exchange ideas and information.

Freehand Kolam

Unlike other forms of kolam, Freehand Kolam is created without the use of any guiding tools or instruments. The artist draws the design freehand, using her fingers to form intricate patterns and

3 - 3   5 - 3   5 - 1   5 - 3

7 - 1   5 - 5   7 - 3

7 - 3   7 - 1   6 - 6

shapes. This requires a great deal of skill and practice, as the artist must be able to maintain the correct proportions and symmetry of the design without any aids. The artist must rely on her creativity, imagination, and skill to create a unique and beautiful design.

The process of creating a Freehand Kolam starts with the artist drawing the design by making a rough outline with her fingers or a stick. From there, she fills in the design with intricate patterns and details. The process requires a great deal of patience and concentration, as mistakes cannot be easily corrected.

Floral Kolam

As the name suggests, Floral Kolam designs are inspired by flowers, and incorporate various floral patterns and shapes. These designs are often intricate and highly detailed and require a great deal of skill and practice to create. Floral Kolam designs can range from simple to complex, depending on the occasion. Some designs incorporate large flowers with detailed petals, while others may feature small clusters of flowers interspersed with leaves and vines. The patterns can also be arranged in various shapes and sizes, such as circular or rectangular.

5 - 1   5 – 3   5 - 3   5 - 3

7 - 1   7 - 3   5 - 5

5 – 5   7 - 1   7 - 3

The colors used in Floral Kolam designs are typically bright and vibrant and are chosen to complement the surrounding environment. The colors used may include a variety of natural hues, including yellows, oranges, pinks, and reds, among others.

Birds and Animals Kolam

Birds and Animals Kolam designs are inspired by various birds and animals found in nature. The designs incorporate various patterns and shapes to create a vivid and detailed representation of the creature. The designs often include images of peacocks, swans, elephants, horses, and other animals that are revered in Hindu mythology. In addition to its aesthetic value, Birds, and Animals Kolam is also steeped in cultural and religious significance. The animals and birds depicted in the designs are often associated with different Hindu deities and are believed to bring good luck and prosperity to the household. They also serve as a way of celebrating and appreciating the natural world. By incorporating images of birds and animals, the kolams pay tribute to the diverse wildlife found in South India and remind us of the importance of preserving and protecting it.

5 - 1   5 - 3   4 - 4   5 - 3

7 - 1   7 - 3   6 − 6

7 − 3   5 - 5   7 - 1

Chapter 5: Kolam in Daily Life

The Beauty of Kolam in Everyday Life

The beauty of kolam lies in its simplicity and the way it can transform even the most mundane spaces into something beautiful and vibrant. In South India, kolam is an integral part of everyday life. It is drawn every day, usually in the morning, to welcome guests and bring good luck and prosperity to the home. Every kolam is unique and reflects the individuality and creativity of the person who created it. One of the most beautiful aspects of kolam is the way it is created using natural materials such as rice flour, chalk powder, and flowers. The designs are made using simple tools such as the fingers, and each stroke is carefully placed to create a beautiful and intricate pattern. The use of natural materials and simple tools gives kolam a sense of purity and authenticity that is unmatched by other art forms. Another aspect of the beauty of kolam is its impermanence. Unlike other art forms that are meant to be preserved for long periods of time, kolam is created anew every day and is washed away by rain or foot traffic. This impermanence is a reminder of the transient nature of life and the importance of living in the present moment.

| 5 - 1 | 5 - 3 | 5 - 3 | 5 - 3 |

| 7 - 1 | 7 - 3 | 5 - 5 |

| 5 - 5 | 7 - 1 | 7 - 3 |

Kolam is not just an art form, it is also a way of life. It is a way to connect with nature, to celebrate the changing seasons, and to mark important occasions such as festivals and weddings. The colors and patterns used in kolam are inspired by nature, and each design has a deeper symbolic meaning. For example, a peacock kolam is believed to bring prosperity and happiness, while a lotus kolam is associated with purity and spiritual awakening.

The beauty of kolam is not just in the final design but in the process of creating it. Drawing a kolam requires patience, skill, and a deep understanding of geometry and symmetry. It is a meditative process that requires focus and concentration and is often used as a form of stress relief. Kolam is not limited to just homes and temples. It is also a common sight on the streets, particularly during festivals such as Diwali and Pongal. The streets are decorated with vibrant and colorful kolams, transforming the entire neighborhood into a festive and joyous atmosphere.

3 - 3   5 - 3   5 - 1   5 - 3

7 - 1   7 - 3   6 - 6

5 - 5   7 - 1   7 - 3

Role of Women in Kolam Tradition

Women play a significant role in the Kolam tradition, which is an intricate art form practiced in South India. For centuries, women have been the primary creators and keepers of this art form, passing it down from generation to generation. The role of women in the Kolam tradition goes beyond just creating decorative patterns but also includes social, cultural, and spiritual aspects.

In South Indian culture, kolam is seen as a woman's domain. It is primarily created by women and is an integral part of their daily routine. Women wake up early in the morning to create kolams in front of their homes as a way to welcome guests and to invite positive energy into their homes. Creating kolam is not just a form of art but also a way for women to express their creativity, spirituality, and cultural identity. Moreover, creating kolam serves as a way for women to socialize and connect with others in the community. Women often gather together to create kolams and exchange ideas and techniques. This fosters a sense of community and togetherness, which is important for mental health and well-being.

| 5 - 3 | 5 - 3 | 5 - 1 | 5 - 3 |

| 7 - 1 | 5 - 5 | 7 - 3 |

| 7 - 3 | 7 - 1 | 5 - 5 |

In addition, women have played a critical role in the preservation and transmission of the kolam tradition from one generation to the next. They have passed down their knowledge and skills to their daughters and granddaughters, ensuring that the art form remains alive and vibrant.

However, despite the central role of women in the kolam tradition, their contributions have often been overlooked and undervalued. Kolam is often seen as a trivial and domestic art form, rather than a complex and sophisticated form of art that requires skill, creativity, and dedication. Women's contributions to the kolam tradition have not been fully recognized, and their skills and expertise have often been dismissed.

Kolam in Weddings and Other Ceremonies

Kolams are an essential part of traditional South Indian weddings and other ceremonies to decorate and beautify the space. Kolams are believed to create positive energy and bring good luck to the event and the people involved. In weddings, kolams are typically drawn in front of the main entrance or the wedding mandap, which is a canopy-like structure where the wedding rituals take place.

5 - 1   5 - 3   4 - 4   5 - 3

7 - 1   7 - 3   6 – 6

5 - 5   7 - 1   7 - 3

The kolams may be simple or elaborate, depending on the family's preferences and the occasion's grandeur. The wedding kolams usually feature traditional motifs like flowers, leaves, birds, and peacocks. These motifs are believed to bring prosperity, happiness, and good fortune to the newlyweds. Some families also include depictions of Hindu gods and goddesses, such as Lord Ganesha, Goddess Lakshmi, and Lord Krishna, to bless the couple.

As a Welcome Sign: Kolams are often used as a way to welcome guests to the wedding or ceremony venue. They are usually drawn at the entrance of the house or venue and serve as a sign of welcome and hospitality.

As a Decorative Element: Kolams are often used as a decorative element in weddings and other ceremonies. They can be drawn on the floor or on a platform and are usually adorned with flowers, candles, and other decorative elements.

As a Symbol of Good Luck: Kolams are believed to bring good luck and prosperity to the household. They are often drawn during weddings and other ceremonies to invoke the blessings of the gods and bring good fortune to the newlyweds or the family.

5 - 1   5 - 3   5 - 3   5 - 3

7 - 1   7 – 3   5 - 5

5 - 5   7 – 1   7 - 3

60

As a Ritualistic Element: In some communities, the act of drawing kolams is considered a ritualistic element of the wedding or ceremony. It is believed to purify the space and ward off evil spirits.

To Showcase Cultural Heritage: Kolams are a unique and beautiful art form that showcase the rich cultural heritage of South India. They are often used in weddings and other ceremonies to celebrate and showcase this heritage.

Kolam as a Means of Storytelling

In South India, kolams are often used to depict scenes from Hindu mythology, folklore, stories, legends, and everyday life. The practice of using Kolam as a means of storytelling has been prevalent for centuries.

In ancient times, women in South Indian villages would draw Kolams in front of their homes as a way of communicating with their neighbors and passing on important messages. For example, a Kolam with a fish design could signify that the fish market was open that day, while a Kolam with a flower design could signify that there was a wedding in the village.

3 - 3   5 - 3   5 - 1   5 - 3

7 - 1   5 - 5   7 - 3

7 - 3   7 - 1   6 - 6

Kolams can be used to tell stories about various deities and their adventures. For example, a kolam featuring Lord Krishna may depict him playing the flute, stealing butter, or engaging in battle with demons. Similarly, a kolam featuring Goddess Lakshmi may depict her showering blessings on the household or distributing wealth and prosperity.

Kolam artists may also use their designs to express their emotions or convey a personal message. For example, a Kolam with a broken heart design may signify heartbreak, while a lotus flower design may signify peace and tranquility. In recent times, kolams have also been used to create awareness about social issues like women's empowerment, environmental conservation, and education. These kolams often feature powerful images and messages that encourage people to act and make a difference.

Kolam as a Social Activity

In South India, Kolam is a common practice among women of all ages and is often done in groups. The act of creating Kolams together promotes socialization, strengthens community bonds, and fosters a sense of belonging.

| 5 - 1 | 5 - 3 | 5 - 3 | 5 - 3 |

| 7 - 1 | 7 - 3 | 5 - 5 |

| 5 - 5 | 7 - 1 | 7 - 3 |

The practice of drawing Kolams together is a way of building community and strengthening social ties. Women may gather in the morning or early evening to draw Kolams in front of their homes or in a common area. Drawing Kolams together also provides an opportunity for women to connect and share their experiences. They may discuss current events, family matters, or simply chat and catch up with each other. Kolam drawing sessions can become a forum for discussing important issues and sharing advice and support.

Kolam drawing sessions may also be an opportunity to learn from each other. Women may share different techniques, patterns, and designs, and learn from each other's experiences. The act of drawing Kolams together can be a way of passing on cultural knowledge and preserving traditional practices.

In addition to being a social activity for women, Kolam is also a way of engaging with the community. During festivals and other special occasions, women may create large and elaborate Kolams in public spaces, inviting others to view and appreciate their art. Kolams can be a way of creating a sense of beauty and festivity in the community and inviting others to participate.

Kolam competitions and festivals are a popular and significant aspect of South Indian culture. These events provide a platform for Kolam artists to showcase their skills and creativity, and for the community to come together and celebrate the art form. Kolam competitions are typically held during festivals or special occasions, such as Pongal, Navratri, or Diwali. Participants may be individuals or teams, and they may compete in various categories, such as traditional, contemporary, or theme based Kolams. The Kolams are judged on criteria such as design, symmetry, color scheme, and technical skill. The winners may receive prizes, trophies, or recognition for their achievements.

Kolam festivals are large-scale events that celebrate the art form and its cultural significance. These festivals may include exhibitions, workshops, demonstrations, and competitions, as well as cultural programs, music, and dance performances. The festivals may be held in public spaces, such as parks or temples, and may attract large crowds of people from different communities.

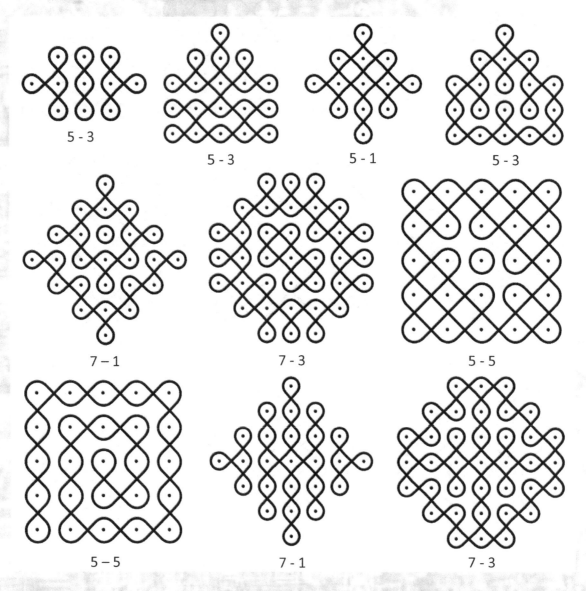

Kolam festivals also provide an opportunity for the community to come together and celebrate. People from different walks of life come to view the Kolams, appreciate the artistry of the artists, and take part in cultural activities and events. Kolam festivals may include music and dance performances, food stalls, and traditional games and activities.

Kolam competitions and festivals have several benefits. They help to preserve and promote the traditional art form, allowing younger generations to learn about and appreciate the significance of Kolam. They also provide a platform for Kolam artists to showcase their skills and gain recognition for their work.

Furthermore, Kolam competitions and festivals help to create a sense of community and belonging. People from different backgrounds and age groups come together to celebrate their cultural heritage and traditions. The events foster a sense of pride and unity among South Indians and help to strengthen social ties.

3 - 3   5 - 3   5 - 1   5 - 3

7 - 1   5 - 5   7 – 3

7 - 3   7 - 1   6 – 6

Chapter 6: Kolam as Art

Kolam and Contemporary Art

Kolam has influenced contemporary art in many ways. The intricate designs, geometric patterns, and use of symmetry in Kolam have inspired contemporary artists to explore and experiment with these elements in their work. The use of bold colors and intricate designs in Kolam has also influenced the use of color and patterns in contemporary art.

Contemporary artists have also been inspired by the process of creating Kolam. The meditative and mindful practice of creating Kolam designs has influenced contemporary artists to incorporate similar techniques in their own work. The repetitive and rhythmic process of creating Kolam designs has been compared to the process of drawing, painting, or sculpting, leading to the development of new techniques and approaches in contemporary art.

5 - 1	5 - 3	5 - 3	5 - 3
7 - 1	7 - 3	5 - 5
5 - 5	7 - 1	7 - 3

In addition, the use of natural materials in creating Kolam designs has influenced contemporary artist to explore sustainable and eco-friendly practices in their work. Some contemporary artists are now using natural and recycled materials, such as leaves, twigs, and recycled paper, to create their work, highlighting the importance of environmental consciousness in contemporary art.

The use of technology and digital tools has also influenced the practice of Kolam. Some contemporary artists are using digital tools to create Kolam designs, leading to the development of new techniques and approaches. The use of technology has also made it possible for Kolam artists to collaborate and share their work with a global audience.

Kolam in the Modern Art World

Kolam has become increasingly significant in the modern art world. Its intricate patterns, cultural significance, and unique beauty have inspired many contemporary artists to incorporate Kolam into their works, helping to preserve and promote this ancient art form. One of the main significances of Kolam in the modern art world is its ability to bridge the gap between tradition and modernity.

5 - 1   5 - 3   4 - 4   5 - 3

7 - 1   5 - 5   7 - 3

7 - 3   7 - 1   6 - 6

By incorporating Kolam into their works, contemporary artists can pay homage to this rich tradition, while also bringing it into the present and making it relevant to modern audiences. Through their works, artists have used Kolam as a means of exploring themes such as gender, identity, cultural exchange, and social issues. This has helped to bring attention to important issues, and to create a space for dialogue and reflection.

Kolam's significance in the modern art world is also reflected in its ability to inspire creativity and innovation. Contemporary artists have experimented with new techniques, materials, and approaches to Kolam, resulting in a diverse range of works that reflect the unique vision and style of each artist. This has helped to expand the boundaries of the art form, and to create new possibilities for its future evolution.

Finally, Kolam's significance in the modern art world is rooted in its ability to connect people across cultural and geographical boundaries. Through its universal themes and motifs, Kolam has become a symbol of cultural exchange and understanding. This has helped to foster a sense of global community, and to promote the values of diversity and inclusivity.

5 - 3   5 - 3   5 - 1   5 - 3

7 - 1   7 - 3   5 - 5

5 - 5   7 - 1   7 - 3

The Use of Kolam in Interior Design

Kolam has found a new avenue for expression in the field of interior design. The use of Kolam in interior design has become increasingly popular as people seek to infuse their homes and living spaces with a touch of cultural authenticity and beauty.

One of the primary ways in which Kolam is used in interior design is as a decorative element on floors. In many South Indian homes, Kolam is traditionally created at the entrance of the house as a way of welcoming guests and to bring good luck and prosperity to the household. In contemporary interior design, Kolam is often incorporated into the flooring as a permanent feature. This can be done using a variety of materials such as tiles, marbles, or even painted designs.

Kolam can also be used as a decorative element on walls. The intricate patterns and designs of Kolam can be used to create stunning murals or wall hangings that add a unique touch of South Indian heritage to a space. This can be done using a variety of materials such as paint, fabric, or even sculpted wood.

| 5 - 1 | 5 - 3 | 4 - 4 | 5 - 3 |

| 7 - 1 | 5 - 5 | 7 - 3 |

| 7 - 3 | 7 - 1 | 6 - 6 |

Another use of Kolam in interior design is as a decorative element in furniture and accessories. Kolam patterns can be incorporated into textiles, such as curtains, pillows, and table runners, to add a touch of color and cultural significance. They can also be used in the design of furniture, such as chairs, tables, and cabinets, to create a unique and personalized look.

Kolam can also be used in lighting design, adding a touch of cultural significance to lamps and light fixtures. The intricate patterns and designs can be etched onto glass, creating a beautiful and unique light diffusion effect.

Apart from being a decorative element, Kolam can also be used to create a sense of spiritual or cultural ambiance. The practice of creating Kolam is deeply rooted in South Indian culture and spirituality. Incorporating Kolam into the design of a space can create a sense of peace, harmony, and connection to one's cultural heritage.

Kolam and Food Art

Kolam has also found its way into the world of food art. The practice of creating Kolam-inspired designs using food has become increasingly popular as people seek to infuse their culinary creations with a touch of cultural authenticity and beauty.

One of the primary ways in which Kolam is incorporated into food art is by using the designs and patterns of Kolam as inspiration for food presentation. Chefs use different colored ingredients, fruits, and vegetables to create intricate patterns and designs that resemble the traditional Kolam designs. For example, watermelon can be sliced and arranged in a circular pattern to resemble a traditional Kolam design.

Kolam is used in food art is as a way of decorating food items such as cakes, desserts, and even savory dishes. Kolam-inspired designs can be created using a variety of edible materials such as frosting, powdered sugar, cocoa powder, or even colored spices. The intricate patterns and designs of Kolam can be used to create stunning visual effects on food items, making them stand out and become a

talking point at any event. The use of Kolam in food art not only adds a unique touch of South Indian heritage to the food, but it also showcases the artist's creativity and skill.

Apart from decorating food items, Kolam-inspired designs can also be created on food plates, table runners, and even tablecloths. This can create a stunning presentation for a meal and add an extra layer of cultural authenticity to the dining experience. Incorporating Kolam into food art also creates an opportunity for cultural exchange. The practice of creating Kolam-inspired designs using food can help people from different cultures learn about and appreciate South Indian art and culture.

The Role of Kolam in Architecture

Kolam, has played a significant role in the architecture of South India. The designs and patterns of Kolam have been used as a source of inspiration for the intricate designs found in temples, palaces, and other architectural structures. In temple architecture, the designs of Kolam are incorporated into the pillars, walls, and ceilings. The intricate patterns and designs are often carved into the stone or painted onto the surface.

5 - 1	5 - 3	7 - 3	5 - 3
7 - 1	7 - 3	5 - 5
5 - 5	7 - 1	7 - 3

These designs not only add beauty to the temple but also serve a spiritual purpose. The patterns and designs are believed to have a positive effect on the energy and atmosphere of the temple, creating a sense of peace and harmony.

In palace architecture, the designs of Kolam are used as inspiration for the intricate and elaborate carvings and decorations found on the walls, ceilings, and pillars. The designs are often geometric and repetitive, creating a sense of symmetry and balance in the overall structure.

Kolam has also influenced the design of traditional South Indian homes. The entrances of homes are often decorated with intricate designs using rice flour or colored powders. These designs not only add a touch of beauty to the home but also serve as a symbol of welcome and hospitality.

Kolam is also used in landscaping to create beautiful and intricate designs in gardens and outdoor spaces. The patterns are created using natural materials such as stones, pebbles, and plants, adding a touch of natural beauty to the space.

5 - 1   5 - 3   4 - 4   5 - 3

7 - 1   5 - 5   7 - 3

7 - 3   7 - 1   6 - 6

In contemporary architecture, the designs, and patterns of Kolam are still being used as a source of inspiration. The intricate patterns and geometric designs of Kolam are being adapted to create modern, innovative structures. The use of Kolam in contemporary architecture is a way of preserving the cultural heritage and traditional art forms of South India while also embracing modernity.

Kolam in Folk Art and Crafts

Kolam has also been incorporated into various forms of folk art and crafts. For instance, Kolam designs are often used to create intricate embroidery patterns on textiles such as sarees, dupattas, and shawls.

One of the most popular folk-art forms that incorporate Kolam is the "Kalamkari" art of Andhra Pradesh and Telangana. Kalamkari is a type of hand-painted or block-printed textile art that uses natural dyes and pigments to create intricate designs and patterns. The designs often include motifs inspired by nature, mythology, and religion, with Kolam being a prominent source of inspiration.

5 - 1   5 - 3   5 - 3   5 - 3

7 - 1   7 - 3   5 - 5

5 - 5   7 - 1   7 - 3

The designs are also used in the creation of traditional South Indian handicrafts such as pottery, wood carving, and basket weaving. The intricate designs of Kolam are often incorporated into the surface of these crafts, creating unique and beautiful pieces. These crafts are not only a way of preserving traditional art forms but also a means of livelihood for many rural communities.

Kolam has been gaining popularity in the world of contemporary art as well. Many artists are incorporating Kolam designs into their artwork, using different mediums such as canvas, paper, and even 3D printing. This has helped in the preservation and promotion of the traditional art form, while also making it accessible to a wider audience.

3 - 3   5 - 3   5 - 1   5 - 3

7 - 1   5 - 5   7 - 3

7 - 3   7 - 1   6 - 6

Chapter 7: Kolam and Culture

Significance of Kolam in Indian Culture

Kolam is an integral part of Indian culture for centuries and has deep religious and social significance.

Cultural Significance: Kolam is a unique art form that has been passed down through generations in South India. It is a way of preserving traditional cultural practices and passing them on to future generations. Kolam is also a way of showcasing the creativity and artistic talent of South Indian women.

Social Significance: Kolam is an important part of social gatherings and festivals in South India. It is often created as a way of celebrating a special occasion or event, such as a wedding, birthday, or religious festival. The act of creating a Kolam is a way of bringing people together and strengthening community bonds.

Educational significance: Kolam is often used as a tool for teaching children about mathematics and geometry. Intricate designs and patterns created in Kolam involve complex mathematical concepts, and children can learn about symmetry, angles, and shapes by creating their own Kolam designs.

Spiritual significance: Kolam is often created in front of homes and temples as a way to invoke the blessings of the gods and goddesses. Intricate designs and patterns created in Kolam are believed to have a spiritual significance and are thought to bring positive energy and good luck to the household.

Ritual significance: Kolam is an important part of many Hindu rituals and festivals. It is often created during special occasions such as weddings, birthdays, and religious festivals, and it is considered a symbol of celebration and joy.

Aesthetical Significance: Kolam is a beautiful form of art that is appreciated for its aesthetic value. The intricate designs and patterns created in Kolam are a testament to the skill and creativity of the artist. Kolam is also a way of beautifying public spaces and adding color and vibrancy to the environment.

5 - 1   5 - 3   4 - 4   5 - 3

7 - 1   5 - 5   7 - 3

7 - 3   7 - 1   6 - 6

Kolam and Cultural Preservation

Kolam is an important part of cultural preservation in the region. Kolam has been passed down from generation to generation for centuries, and it reflects the rich cultural heritage of the region. Here are some of the ways Kolam is helping to preserve South Indian culture:

Passing on traditional knowledge: Kolam is often taught from mother to daughter, and it is an important way of passing on traditional knowledge and skills. By teaching their daughters how to create Kolam, mothers are helping to preserve the art form and ensure that it is passed on to future generations.

Celebrating cultural identity: Kolam is an integral part of the cultural identity of South India. By creating Kolam designs in front of their homes and temples, people are celebrating their cultural identity and express their pride in their heritage.

Maintaining community connections: Creating Kolam is often a communal activity, with women coming together to create the designs. This helps to maintain community connections and strengthen social bonds, which are important for cultural preservation.

Engaging with younger generations: Kolam is a way of engaging with younger generations and introducing them to traditional art forms. By teaching children how to create Kolam, older generations are helping to keep the art form alive and ensure that it continues to be passed down to future generations.

Supporting local economies: Kolam is often created using locally sourced materials such as rice flour and chalk powder. By supporting local businesses and economies, people are helping to preserve the traditional practices and customs that are important for cultural preservation.

Kolam and Cultural Exchange

Kolam has been influenced by various cultures over the years. The art form has been influenced by different regions, religions, and communities, resulting in a diverse range of styles and designs. For example, the Kolams created in Tamil Nadu are different from the ones created in Kerala or Andhra Pradesh. Similarly, the Kolams created during Hindu festivals are different from the ones created during Muslim or Christian festivals.

3 - 3	5 - 3	5 - 1	5 - 3
7 - 1	5 - 5	7 - 3
7 – 3	7 - 1	6 - 6

Kolam has also served as a medium for cultural exchange between different communities. Kolam competitions and exhibitions are held across India and the world, bringing together people from different backgrounds and cultures. These events allow people to appreciate the beauty of Kolam and learn about the cultural heritage of South India. It also provides an opportunity for people from different cultures to exchange ideas and learn from each other.

Moreover, Kolam is a way of preserving and promoting cultural diversity. By spreading the art of Kolam to other parts of India and the world, South Indians are also promoting their culture and values. It also helps in breaking down cultural barriers and promoting cross-cultural understanding and appreciation. Kolam workshops and exhibitions have been organized in many parts of the world, including the United States, Japan, and Europe. Through these events, people from different cultures have been introduced to the art of Kolam and have been able to appreciate its beauty and cultural significance. Similarly, South Indian Kolam artists have had the opportunity to showcase their art and share their cultural heritage with people from different parts of the world.

4 – 4   5 - 3   5 - 1   5 - 3

7 – 1   7 - 3   5 - 5

5 – 5   7 - 1   7 - 3

Regional Variations in Kolam

While the basic principles of Kolam remain the same, the style and design of Kolam vary greatly across different regions of South India. Each region has its unique style, patterns, and motifs that reflect the cultural identity of the community.

Here are some of the regional variations in Kolam:

Tamil Nadu Kolam: Tamil Nadu is known for its intricate and geometric designs in Kolam. The designs usually have a square or rectangular base, and intricate lines and dots are added to create patterns.

Andhra Pradesh Kolam: In Andhra Pradesh, Kolam is known as Muggu. The designs are usually made up of curved lines and circles and are more fluid and organic than the ones in Tamil Nadu. They also use a wide range of colors.

Kerala Kolam: Kolam in Kerala is called Pookalam and is created using flower petals instead of rice flour or chalk powder. The designs are typically floral and have a circular or spiral pattern.

5 - 1   5 - 3   4 - 4   5 - 3

7 - 1   5 - 5   7 - 3

7 - 3   7 - 1   6 - 6

Karnataka Kolam: In Karnataka, Kolam is known as Rangoli or Hase and is similar to the ones created in Tamil Nadu. The designs are usually made up of straight lines and geometric shapes and are more symmetrical and structured.

Maharashtra Kolam: In Maharashtra, Kolam is known as Raangolee or Haldi Kumkum. The designs are usually made up of floral and geometric patterns and use a wide range of colors.

Gujarat Kolam: In Gujarat, Kolam is known as Chowk Purna or Sathiya or Rangoli. The designs are usually made up of intricate patterns and motifs, and the colors used are bright and vibrant.

In Punjab, Haryana, Himachal Pradesh, and parts of Uttar Pradesh it is called Chowk-poorana or Chowkpurana. Alpana in Bengal, Chowk Pujan in Bihar and Madhya Pradesh, Osa in Odisha, Mandana in Rajasthan, etc.

Kolam Across Borders

Although Kolam is predominantly practiced in South India, the art form has also gained popularity in other parts of the country and even beyond India's borders.

| 3 - 3 | 5 - 3 | 5 - 1 | 5 - 3 |

| 7 - 1 | 7 - 3 | 5 - 5 |

| 5 - 5 | 7 - 1 | 7 - 3 |

Over time, the practice of Kolam has spread to other parts of India, including Maharashtra, Gujarat, and West Bengal. While its roots lie in South India, the practice of Kolam has spread to other countries, including Malaysia, Singapore, Indonesia, Sri Lanka, and even the United States.

In Malaysia, Kolam is a common sight in Indian households and is often created during festivals and weddings. The designs are similar to those found in South India, and they are usually created using colored rice, flowers, and leaves. In Singapore, the practice of Kolam is mostly limited to the Indian community, and it is usually created using colored sand or rice flour. Kolam is also used to decorate temples and community centers during festivals and cultural events.

In Indonesia, Kolam is known as Rangoli, and it is often created during the Diwali festival. The designs are inspired by traditional Indian motifs and patterns and are created using colored sand, rice flour, or flower petals.

In Sri Lanka, Kolam is known as Kola, and it is usually created using colored rice flour. The designs are similar to those found in South India, and they are created to celebrate festivals and special occasions.

5 - 1   5 - 3   4 - 4   5 - 3

7 - 1   5 - 5   7 - 3

7 - 3   7 - 1   6 - 6

In the United States, Kolam has gained popularity among the Indian American community. Artists in the US have adapted the art form to suit their environment and materials, using colored sand, chalk, or even paint to create their designs. Kolam has also become a means of social and cultural exchange, with workshops and classes being held to teach the art form to people of all backgrounds.

In Europe, Kolam has also gained popularity among the Indian diaspora and local communities. Artists in countries such as the UK and France have created their own versions of Kolam, using materials such as chalk, sand, or flower petals. The designs often incorporate traditional motifs and patterns, and they are used to decorate homes, temples, and public spaces.

The popularity of Kolam across borders is a testament to the beauty and significance of this traditional art form. It reflects the diversity and richness of Indian culture and serves as a bridge between different communities and cultures.

5 - 1   5 - 3   4 - 4   5 - 3

7 - 1   7 - 3   5 - 5

5 - 5   7 - 1   7 - 3

Kolam and Globalization

   Globalization has had a significant impact on the practice of Kolam. As the world becomes more connected, traditional art forms such as Kolam have gained wider recognition and appreciation beyond their local communities. At the same time, the influence of globalization has also brought new materials, techniques, and inspirations to the practice of Kolam. With the advent of technology and social media, the practice of Kolam has become more accessible to a global audience. Artists from different parts of the world can now share their designs and techniques online, creating a space for cross-cultural exchange and collaboration. This has led to the emergence of new styles and techniques in Kolam, as artists draw inspiration from different cultures and traditions. However, globalization has also brought challenges to the practice of Kolam. With the rise of modernization and urbanization, traditional art forms such as Kolam have faced the risk of being forgotten or marginalized. This has led to efforts to preserve and promote traditional art forms, including Kolam, through education, documentation, and cultural festivals.

3 – 3   5 - 3   4 - 4   5 - 1

7 – 1   5 - 5   7 - 3

7 – 3   7 - 1   6 - 6

Chapter 8: Kolam and Mathematics

Kolam and Mathematics

Kolam, is not only a beautiful expression of creativity and cultural heritage but also an intriguing subject of mathematics. The intricate patterns and geometric shapes of Kolam are based on mathematical principles, making it a fascinating subject for those interested in both art and mathematics.

The basic building blocks of a Kolam are dots and lines. The dots are placed in a specific pattern, and then lines are drawn to connect them, creating intricate geometric shapes. Many Kolam designs are based on simple geometric shapes, such as squares, triangles, and circles, which are repeated and combined to create intricate patterns. The designs often feature geometric transformations, such as reflections, rotations, and translations, which create symmetry and balance.

The mathematics of Kolam is particularly interesting in terms of symmetry. Kolams are often created using reflection and rotation, and the use of these symmetry operations can be studied mathematically. Kolam designs may use rotational symmetry, where the design looks the same when rotated around a centre point, or reflectional symmetry, where the design looks the same when reflected across a line. Symmetry operations can be represented using matrices, and the properties of these matrices can be analysed to understand the symmetry of the Kolam.

The study of Kolam can also involve the use of number theory. The number of dots used in a Kolam can be analysed using number theory concepts, such as prime numbers and divisibility. The placement of dots can be based on different mathematical series, such as Fibonacci and Lucas series, creating different types of Kolam designs. Furthermore, the use of symmetry and repetition in Kolam can be linked to concepts of tessellation and fractals in mathematics. Tessellation involves the repetition of shapes to cover a surface without gaps or overlaps, and this is often seen in Kolam designs. Fractals are self-similar patterns that repeat at different scales, and they are found in many natural forms, such as trees, snowflakes, and coastlines.

3 - 3   5 - 3   5 - 1   4 - 4

7 - 1   5 - 5   7 - 3

7 - 3   7 - 1   6 - 6

The Role of Geometry in Kolam

Geometry plays a crucial role in the creation of Kolam. Kolam designs are based on grids, dots, and lines, which follow certain geometric principles. The use of geometry in Kolam designs gives them a sense of order and symmetry, making them visually pleasing and aesthetically pleasing.

One of the most fundamental elements of Kolam is the use of dots. Dots are used as a base for creating the design, and their placement and number determine the final shape of the Kolam. The dots are usually placed in a grid pattern, and the number of dots in each row and column determines the symmetry of the design. By analysing the placement of dots, mathematicians and researchers can understand the underlying geometric principles behind Kolam designs.

Lines are another important element of Kolam. They are used to connect the dots and create the design. The lines used in Kolam designs are usually straight, but sometimes curved lines are also used. The use of geometric patterns in Kolam designs is not limited to dots and lines. Other geometric shapes such as triangles, circles, and squares are also used to create designs. These shapes are arranged in a repeating pattern, which creates a sense of order and symmetry in the design.

3 - 3	5 - 3	4 - 4	5 - 1
7 - 1	5 - 5	7 - 3
7 - 3	7 - 1	6 - 6

The Concept of Sacred Geometry

Sacred geometry is a concept that describes the relationship between geometry and spirituality. It is the idea that certain geometric shapes and patterns have symbolic or spiritual meaning and can be used to connect with a higher power or cosmic energy. This concept has been around for thousands of years and can be found in many cultures, including ancient Egypt, Greece, and India. For example, many ancient temples and cathedrals were built using sacred geometry to create a sacred space that would inspire worship and contemplation.

The principles of sacred geometry are based on the belief that there is a universal language of geometric shapes that can be used to describe and understand the underlying structure of the universe. This language includes shapes such as the circle, square, triangle, and spiral, as well as more complex shapes such as the dodecahedron and the flower of life. In sacred geometry, certain shapes and symbols are believed to represent fundamental aspects of the universe and the divine.

3 - 3   5 - 1   5 - 3   4 - 4

7 - 1   5 - 5   7 - 3

7 - 3   7 - 1   6 - 6

One of the most common shapes found in sacred geometry is the circle, which represents unity, wholeness, and infinity. The circle is also often used to represent the cycle of life and death, as well as the cyclical nature of the universe.

Another common shape is the triangle, which is often associated with the concept of the Trinity in Christianity and represents balance and harmony. The triangle is also used in many other spiritual traditions, such as Hinduism and Buddhism, where it is seen as a symbol of the union between the body, mind, and spirit. Other shapes, such as the square, pentagon, and hexagon, are also used in various contexts and carry their own meanings.

One of the most well-known examples of sacred geometry is the golden ratio, also known as the divine proportion. This mathematical ratio is found in nature, art, and architecture, and is believed to have a harmonious and aesthetically pleasing effect on the human psyche.

The flower of life is another important shape in sacred geometry. It is a complex pattern made up of overlapping circles that is believed to hold the secrets of the universe. It is often used as a meditation tool and is said to help people connect with their higher selves.

90

Sacred geometry is also often associated with the practice of feng shui, which is the ancient Chinese art of arranging spaces to create a harmonious and balanced environment. By using principles of sacred geometry, feng shui practitioners believe they can create spaces that promote health, prosperity, and spiritual well-being.

While the concept of sacred geometry has been around for thousands of years, it continues to inspire and influence people today. Many people use sacred geometry in their spiritual practices, such as meditation or yoga, to connect with the divine and achieve a deeper understanding of the universe. Others use it in their creative pursuits, using the principles of sacred geometry to create art and designs that are both aesthetically pleasing and spiritually meaningful.

The Concept of Fractals

The patterns used in Kolam often incorporate fractal geometry, which allows for the creation of complex and beautiful designs that repeat at different scales. The use of fractals in Kolam is based on the principle of self-similarity, which is a key characteristic of fractals.

3 - 3   5 - 3   4 - 4   5 - 3

7 - 1   5 - 5   7 - 3

7 - 3   7 - 1   6 - 6

This means that the same pattern can be found within itself, no matter how small or large it is. For example, a smaller triangle in a Kolam design may be similar in shape to the larger triangle that it is a part of, creating a self-similar pattern that repeats at different scales.

Fractals are found in nature, art, and science, and they are an important part of many fields, including physics, computer graphics, and chaos theory. The concept of fractals was first introduced by Benoit Mandelbrot in the 1970s. Mandelbrot was a mathematician who was interested in finding patterns in complex systems. He discovered that many natural phenomena, such as coastlines, mountains, and clouds, could be described using fractals. Mandelbrot developed a set of mathematical equations that could be used to generate fractals, and he used computer graphics to create images of these patterns.

One of the key features of fractals is their self-similarity. This means that a fractal pattern looks the same at different levels of magnification. For example, a fern leaf is a fractal because it has the same basic shape and pattern at different levels of magnification. If you look at a small part of the leaf, you will see that it has the same basic shape and pattern as the entire leaf.

3 - 1   5 - 3   5 - 1   5 - 3

7 - 1   5 - 5   7 - 3

7 - 3   7 - 1   5 - 5

Fractals can be described using mathematical equations. One of the most famous fractals is the Mandelbrot set, which is generated using a simple equation. The Mandelbrot set is a complex, intricate pattern that is self-similar at different scales. It has become a popular subject for computer-generated art and has inspired many artists and mathematicians.

Fractals are not just found in nature and art. They are also used in science and technology. For example, fractals are used to describe the behaviour of complex systems, such as the weather or the stock market. They are also used in computer graphics to create realistic images of natural phenomena, such as clouds or mountains.

The use of fractals in Kolam allows for the creation of designs that are both intricate and beautiful, while also being relatively simple to create. The use of fractals in Kolam art reflects the traditional Indian belief in the interconnectedness of all things. The repeating patterns of fractals are seen as a metaphor for the way that all things in the universe are connected, and the practice of creating Kolam art is seen as a way of expressing this interconnectedness.

The Concept of Infinity

The concept of infinity is one of the most fascinating and perplexing ideas in mathematics and philosophy. It refers to the idea of something being limitless, boundless, or never-ending. The concept of infinity has been studied and explored for thousands of years, and it has led to many important discoveries and advancements in mathematics and science. While the concept of infinity is not explicitly expressed in Kolam, it can be seen in the use of repetitive patterns that continue indefinitely. The use of repetition and symmetry in Kolam reflects the idea of infinity, as the patterns created can continue infinitely in all directions. The use of dots, lines, and curves to create intricate patterns is a form of visual poetry that expresses the interconnectedness of all things, a key tenet of Indian philosophy.

The infinite patterns in Kolam are seen as a metaphor for the infinite nature of the universe, and the practice of creating Kolam art is seen as a way of expressing this interconnectedness. The concept of infinity in Kolam art also has spiritual significance. Many of the patterns used in Kolam have been passed down through generations and are steeped in traditional symbolism.

For example, the lotus flower is a common motif in Kolam art and represents purity and spiritual awakening. The infinite nature of the lotus pattern reflects the idea that spiritual growth and enlightenment are ongoing processes that have no end.

The patterns created in Kolam are not static but are dynamic, changing over time as the rice flour or chalk powder is blown away or trampled on by people walking over them. This transient nature of Kolam reflects the impermanence of life and the idea that all things are in a state of constant flux.

In this way, the concept of infinity in Kolam is not a literal or mathematical one, but rather a philosophical and spiritual one. It is a reminder of the interconnectedness of all things and the impermanence of life, and it serves as a form of meditation and contemplation for those who create and observe Kolam art.

3 - 3   5 - 3   4 - 4   5 - 3

7 - 1   5 - 5   7 - 3

7 - 3   7 - 1   6 - 6

The Concept of Impermanence

The concept of impermanence is a fundamental idea in many philosophical and spiritual traditions, including Buddhism, Taoism, and Hinduism. It refers to the idea that all things are temporary and subject to change, and that nothing in the physical world is permanent or unchanging.

In Buddhism, the concept of impermanence is known as "anicca" and is one of the three universal characteristics of existence, along with suffering and non-self. The Buddha taught that everything in the physical world, including our bodies, thoughts, and emotions, is impermanent and constantly changing. By recognizing the impermanence of all things, we can develop a sense of detachment and freedom from attachment and craving.

Similarly, in Taoism, the concept of impermanence is seen as a natural part of the cycle of life and death. The Taoist belief in the Tao, or the natural way of the universe, emphasizes the importance of living in harmony with the natural world and accepting the impermanence of all things.

In Hinduism, the concept of impermanence is expressed through the idea of "maya," which refers to the illusory nature of the physical world. According to Hindu philosophy, the physical world is an illusion that is constantly changing and is ultimately impermanent. The goal of spiritual practice is to transcend the illusory nature of the physical world and realize the eternal nature of the self.

The transience of Kolam is a reflection of the Buddhist concept of impermanence. The patterns and designs created in Kolam are not meant to last forever, but rather to be enjoyed in the present moment and then allowed to disappear. This is a powerful reminder that everything in life is temporary and subject to change.

The ephemeral nature of Kolam also emphasizes the importance of mindfulness and living in the present moment. Kolam artists must be fully present and focused on their work as they create their designs, knowing that they will soon be gone. This sense of impermanence encourages people to appreciate the beauty of the moment and to cultivate a sense of gratitude and mindfulness.

3 - 3   5 - 3   4 - 4   5 - 3

7 - 1   5 - 5   7 - 3

7 - 3   7 - 1   6 - 6

Another aspect of Kolam that reflects the concept of impermanence is the way it is created. Kolam patterns are not drawn using a pencil or a pen, but rather by connecting dots and lines with the fingers. This tactile approach to creating art emphasizes the importance of physical presence and the temporary nature of our bodies.

The Concept of Balance

The concept of balance is an important idea in many philosophical and spiritual traditions, including Taoism, Buddhism, and Hinduism. It refers to the idea of maintaining a harmonious equilibrium between different aspects of life and the universe.

In Taoism, the concept of balance is expressed through the idea of yin and yang, which are opposite but complementary forces that are present in all things. According to Taoist philosophy, the key to a harmonious life is to maintain a balance between yin and yang, which can be achieved through practices like meditation, martial arts, and acupuncture.

5 - 3   5 - 3   3 - 3   5 - 3

7 - 1   5 - 5   7 - 3

7 - 3   7 - 1   6 - 6

Similarly, in Buddhism, the concept of balance is emphasized through the idea of the Middle Way, which refers to the path between extreme self-indulgence and extreme self-denial. The Buddha taught that the key to a balanced life is to avoid the extremes of pleasure and pain and to cultivate a sense of mindfulness and detachment.

In Hinduism, the concept of balance is expressed through the idea of dharma, which refers to the cosmic order of the universe. According to Hindu philosophy, the key to a balanced life is to live in harmony with dharma, which involves fulfilling one's duties and responsibilities and living a virtuous life.

The concept of balance is an integral part of Kolam. The intricate patterns and designs created in Kolam are a beautiful expression of the idea of harmonious equilibrium and the importance of balance in our lives. In Kolam, the concept of balance is expressed through the use of symmetrical patterns and designs. These designs are carefully crafted to create a sense of visual harmony and balance, with each element of the design complementing and balancing the other.

3 - 3   5 - 3   4 - 4   5 - 3

7 - 1   5 - 5   7 - 3

7 - 3   7 - 1   6 - 6

The materials used in Kolam also reflect the concept of balance. Rice flour or chalk powder is used to create the intricate designs, and the act of creating the Kolam requires a delicate balance between precision and fluidity. The artist must be able to balance their movements and maintain a steady hand to create the intricate patterns and designs.

Additionally, the act of creating a Kolam requires a sense of balance between tradition and innovation. While Kolam is a traditional art form that has been passed down through generations, each artist also brings their own unique style and creativity to their work. The balance between tradition and innovation is a key aspect of Kolam, and it reflects the importance of balancing our connection to the past with our need for progress and innovation.

The Concept of Interconnectedness

The concept of interconnectedness, also known as interdependence, is the idea that everything in the universe is connected and dependent on each other. This concept can be found in many philosophical and spiritual traditions, including Buddhism, Taoism, and Hinduism.

3 - 3   5 - 3   4 - 4   5 - 3

7 - 1   5 - 5   7 - 3

7 - 3   7 - 1   6 - 6

In Buddhism, the concept of interconnectedness is expressed through the idea of dependent origination, which teaches that all phenomena arise in dependence upon other phenomena. This means that everything in the universe is interconnected and dependent on each other, and that no phenomenon can exist independently or in isolation.

In Taoism, the concept of interconnectedness is expressed through the idea of the Tao, which is the ultimate reality that underlies all existence. According to Taoist philosophy, the Tao is present in all things, and everything in the universe is interconnected and interdependent.

In Hinduism, the concept of interconnectedness is expressed through the idea of Bramham, which is the ultimate reality that underlies all existence. According to Hindu philosophy, everything in the universe is interconnected and dependent on Bramham, and the goal of spiritual practice is to realize this interconnectedness and merge with Bramham.

3 - 3 5 - 3 4 - 4 5 - 3

7 - 1 5 - 5 7 - 3

7 - 3 7 - 1 6 - 6

The concept of interconnectedness has important implications for our understanding of the world and our place in it. It reminds us that we are all connected and that our actions have an impact on others and the world around us. It also encourages us to cultivate a sense of compassion and empathy towards others, as we are all part of the same interconnected web of existence.

In the art of Kolam, the concept of interconnectedness is expressed through the intricate designs and patterns that are created. Each element of the design is connected to the others, and the overall design is a beautiful expression of the idea of interdependence and interconnectedness. By creating these intricate designs, Kolam artists remind us of the importance of recognizing our interconnectedness with others and the world around us.

Chapter 9: Kolam and Society

Kolam and Environmental Awareness

Kolam has a close connection with environmental awareness. Some of the ways in which Kolam promotes environmental awareness:

Use of natural materials: Kolam was created using natural materials like rice flour and natural dyes made from flowers, leaves, and other organic matter. By using these materials, artists demonstrate a respect for the environment and an awareness of the importance of sustainable practices.

Minimal waste: The practice of creating Kolam involves minimal waste. The materials used to create Kolam are biodegradable and easily decompose, which means they do not contribute to landfills or other environmental issues.

3 - 3   5 - 3   5 - 1   4 - 4

7 - 1   5 – 5   7 - 3

7 - 3   7 - 1   6 - 6

Promotes biodiversity: Many Kolam designs incorporate natural elements like flowers and leaves, which promotes biodiversity by encouraging the growth and protection of these natural resources. This can contribute to the overall health and sustainability of ecosystem.

Mindful consumption: Creating Kolam is a mindful practice that requires concentration, patience, and attention to detail. This encourages a mindful approach to consumption and promotes a culture of reducing waste and living sustainably.

Environmental messages: Some Kolam designs incorporate environmental messages, such as messages about the importance of conservation or protecting the environment. These messages can help raise awareness and encourage people to take action to protect the environment.

Eco-friendly practices: In addition to using natural materials, Kolam artists also practice eco-friendly techniques. For example, after creating a Kolam, the materials used are often given to animals and birds as food. This promotes a circular economy and minimizes waste.

Inspiration for eco-friendly initiatives: Kolam has also inspired eco-friendly initiatives in other areas. For example, some schools and organizations have started using Kolam as a way to promote environmental awareness and eco-friendly practices.

3 - 3	5 - 3	5 - 1	5 - 3
7 - 1	5 - 5	7 - 3	
7 - 3	7 - 1	6 - 6	

The Role of Kolam in Education

kolam also plays a significant role in education, particularly in the early childhood years. Kolam can be used as a teaching tool to develop several skills, such as creativity, concentration, problem-solving, and fine motor skills.

Creativity: Kolam is a highly creative art form that allows individuals to express themselves through their designs. Children can use Kolam as a platform to showcase their creativity and imagination. They can experiment with different colors, patterns, and shapes to create unique designs.

Math and Geometry: Kolams are highly geometric in nature, and the creation of a Kolam requires a good understanding of basic geometric shapes and their properties. Children can learn about geometric concepts such as symmetry, congruence, and angles through the process of creating Kolams. They can also practice their math skills by counting the number of dots and lines used in the design.

3 - 3   5 - 3   4 - 4   5 - 3

7 - 1   5 - 5   7 - 3

7 - 3   7 - 1   6 - 6

Concentration: Creating a kolam requires focus and concentration. Children need to pay attention to detail and follow a particular pattern. This helps improve their concentration and attention span, which is crucial for learning.

Problem-solving: Creating a kolam requires planning and problem-solving skills. Children need to figure out how to create a design that is aesthetically pleasing and balanced. They also need to think on their feet and make adjustments if they make a mistake.

Fine motor skills: Drawing a kolam requires fine motor skills, such as hand-eye coordination, finger dexterity, and control. These skills are essential for activities such as writing, drawing, and painting.

Social Skills: Creating Kolams can be a collaborative effort, with different family members or friends working together to create a design. This can help children develop important social skills such as communication, cooperation, and teamwork.

Cultural Heritage: Kolam is an important part of the cultural heritage of South India. By learning about Kolam, children can gain a deeper appreciation of their cultural roots and traditions. They can also learn about the different meanings and symbolism behind different Kolam designs.

5 - 3   5 - 3   3 - 3   5 - 3

7 - 1   5 - 5   7 - 3

7 – 3   7 - 1   6 - 6

Kolam and Gender Issues

Traditionally, kolam-making has been a female-dominated activity. This has also led to a perception that kolam-making is a women's activity and that men should not be involved in it. This has resulted in gender stereotypes and has limited the participation of men in kolam-making. Men are often discouraged from taking up kolam-making as a hobby or as a means of earning an income. This has resulted in a lack of diversity in the kolam-making community and has limited opportunities for men to express their artistic talents.

Kolam-making is considered a domestic chore assigned to women and not recognized as a skilled art form. Women who create kolams face several challenges, including lack of recognition and limited opportunities to showcase their work. Moreover, women who create kolams are often not adequately compensated for their work. They are paid a nominal fee for their services, which is not commensurate with the time and effort they put into creating intricate designs. In recent years, there have been efforts to promote kolam-making as a form of art and recognize the contributions of women who create kolams.

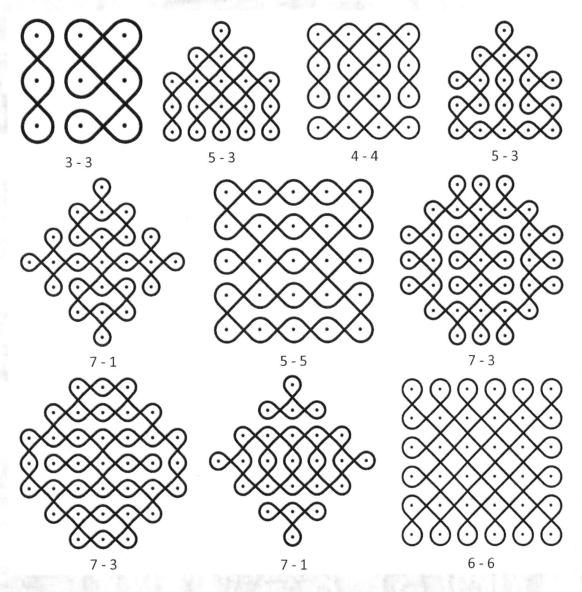

3 - 3	5 - 3	4 - 4	5 - 3
7 - 1	5 - 5	7 - 3	
7 - 3	7 - 1	6 - 6	

Several organizations have been set up to provide training and support to women who create kolams. This has helped women gain recognition and appreciation for their artistic talents.

Kolam and Tourism

Kolam has gained significant popularity in recent years, not only as a traditional art form but also as a tourist attraction. The intricate designs and patterns draw the attention of tourists who are eager to learn about the history and significance of the art form. In many parts of South India, kolam-making has become a part of the tourist itinerary, with several organized tours and workshops dedicated to teaching the art form.

Tourists can witness the process of creating Kolam, which involves a lot of skill, patience, and creativity. They can also learn about the significance of different patterns and symbols used in Kolam, and how they relate to local customs and traditions. The growing interest in kolam-making among tourists has also led to the development of new business opportunities.

108

Local artisans and entrepreneurs have started organizing kolam-making classes and workshops for tourists, offering them an opportunity to learn the art form and create their own kolams. Some hotels and resorts have also started offering kolam-making classes as part of their cultural activities, providing tourists with a unique and immersive experience of the local culture.

Kolam is also an integral part of many festivals and ceremonies in South India, and tourists can witness the creation of elaborate and beautiful Kolams during these occasions. During festivals such as Pongal, Diwali, and Navaratri, the streets of South India come alive with colorful Kolams. These festivals provide an opportunity for tourists to witness the cultural richness of South India and immerse themselves in the local traditions.

Many tour operators in South India offer Kolam tours that take tourists to different villages and towns to witness the creation of Kolams. These tours are usually led by local women who are experts in the art form and can provide insights into the history and significance of Kolam. Tourists can also participate in workshops where they can learn to create their own Kolams under the guidance of local experts.

109

The promotion of kolam-making as a tourist attraction has also helped to preserve and promote the art form. The increased demand for kolam-making has encouraged local artisans to continue practicing and passing on their knowledge to future generations. This, in turn, has helped to preserve the traditional art form and prevent it from becoming extinct.

Kolam and Community Building

Kolam has been used as a tool for community building for centuries. Kolam is a communal activity that involves women of all ages coming together to create beautiful designs. This practice creates a sense of camaraderie and fosters a community spirit among the women who participate. Women who create Kolams share their knowledge and skills with younger generations, passing down the tradition from generation to generation. The practice also serves as a way for women to share their experiences, exchange ideas and support one another.

In many communities in South India, Kolam is seen as a way to build and strengthen social ties. The creation of Kolams in front of houses is not just limited to family members; neighbors and friends also participate in the activity. The practice of Kolam often leads to impromptu conversations and social interactions between neighbors, fostering a sense of community and togetherness.

Kolam has also been used as a tool for community development and social change. In some villages, Kolam competitions and exhibitions are held to promote the art form and bring people together. These events often attract large crowds, and the proceeds from them are used for community development initiatives such as building schools or providing healthcare facilities. The art form has also been used to promote environmental awareness, with some communities creating Kolams that promote sustainability and ecological conservation. The practice of creating Kolams is also used to impart cultural values and traditions to younger generations.

5 - 1   5 - 3   4 - 4   5 - 3

7 - 1   5 - 5   7 - 3

7 - 3   7 - 1   6 - 6

Kolam competitions and exhibitions are also an integral part of community building in South India. These events bring people from different communities and regions together, providing an opportunity for cultural exchange and learning. Participants in these competitions are often judged not just on the aesthetic appeal of their Kolams but also on the cultural significance and the story behind them, promoting an appreciation of cultural heritage and diversity.

The use of social media has also played a significant role in community building through Kolam. Many people, particularly women, have started sharing their Kolam creations on social media platforms, creating a virtual community of Kolam enthusiasts. This online community has provided a platform for people to share their knowledge and experiences, exchange ideas, and showcase their creativity, promoting a sense of community even among those who are physically distant.

Chapter 10: Kolam and Health

Kolam as a Meditative Practice

Beyond their decorative function, kolams are also considered a form of meditation and mindfulness practice. Creating a kolam requires focus, patience, and attention to detail, which can help calm the mind and bring about a sense of inner peace. The repetitive nature of drawing the designs can also have a soothing effect on the nervous system and help to reduce stress.

Kolam is usually drawn early in the morning, before the sun rises, as a way of welcoming the day and invoking positive energy. The process of creating the design requires focus, attention to detail, and a calm state of mind. As the pattern takes shape, the Kolam artist becomes absorbed in the creative process, forgetting their worries and troubles. It is a form of mindfulness, where one is fully present in the moment, and the mind is free from distractions.

3 - 3	5 - 3	4 - 4	5 - 3
7 - 1	5 - 5	7 - 3	
7 - 3	7 - 1	6 - 6	

Kolam is also a social activity, where women in the community come together to create intricate designs. They share stories, exchange ideas, and strengthen their bonds while drawing Kolam. It is a way of connecting with others and building a sense of community. In many households, children learn the art of Kolam from their mothers or grandmothers, passing down the tradition from one generation to another.

The beauty of Kolam lies in its impermanence. The patterns are drawn on the ground and are washed away at the end of the day, symbolizing the impermanence of life. It teaches us to embrace the present moment and appreciate the beauty in the fleeting nature of things.

Kolam and Mental Health

Kolam has been used as a therapeutic tool for people with mental health conditions such as depression and anxiety. It has been found to help improve mood, increase self-esteem, and promote a sense of calm. The repetitive nature of drawing Kolam patterns can also have a calming effect, similar to that of other meditative practices such as yoga and meditation.

Here are some ways in which Kolam can benefit mental health:

Stress relief: Drawing Kolam can be a relaxing and calming activity that can help reduce stress levels. The repetitive nature of drawing the patterns can be meditative and help calm the mind.

Mindfulness: Kolam is a form of mindfulness practice where one is fully present in the moment and focused on the task at hand. This can help increase awareness and decrease distractions, leading to a greater sense of calm and inner peace.

Improved mood: The act of creating something beautiful can be a mood booster. Drawing Kolam can be a source of creative expression that can bring a sense of accomplishment and satisfaction.

Social connection: Kolam is often a social activity, where people come together to draw patterns and share stories. This can help build social connections and a sense of community, which is important for mental health.

3 - 3   5 - 3   4 - 4   5 - 3

7 - 1   5 - 5   7 - 3

7 - 3   7 - 1   6 - 6

Cognitive stimulation: Drawing Kolam can also be a cognitive stimulation activity, where one can improve their problem-solving skills and enhance their creativity.

Mindfulness-based interventions have been shown to be effective in reducing symptoms of depression, anxiety, and stress. By incorporating Kolam into these interventions, practitioners can engage in a mindful and creative practice that promotes mental wellbeing.

Kolam and Physical Exercise

The process of drawing Kolam can involve physical movements such as squatting, bending, and walking around the design. Here are some ways in which Kolam can benefit physical health:

Hand-eye coordination: Drawing Kolam requires hand-eye coordination to create the intricate designs accurately. This can help improve coordination between the hands and the eyes, which is essential for many everyday activities.

3 - 3	5 - 3	4 - 4	5 - 3
7 - 1	5 - 5	7 - 3	
7 - 3	7 - 1	6 - 6	

Fine motor skills: Drawing Kolam involves using fine motor skills to create small, intricate patterns. These skills can be essential for many activities such as writing, typing, and even self-care tasks such as brushing teeth and getting dressed.

Cardiovascular health: Drawing Kolam can be a moderate physical activity that can help improve cardiovascular health. The physical movements involved can increase heart rate and breathing, leading to improved blood circulation.

Improves mobility: Physical movements involved in drawing Kolam can help improve mobility and flexibility. Squatting and bending can help strengthen leg muscles and improve joint flexibility.

Increases activity levels: Drawing Kolam can be a way to increase activity levels, especially for those who have a sedentary lifestyle. Walking around the design, stretching, and squatting can help burn calories and improve overall fitness.

Low-impact exercise: Drawing Kolam is a low-impact exercise that is gentle on joints and suitable for people of all ages. It can be a great alternative to high-impact exercises that can be hard on the body.

3 - 3   5 - 3   4 - 4   5 - 3

7 - 1   5 - 5   7 - 3

7 - 3   7 - 1   6 - 6

Full-body workout: Drawing Kolam involves getting up and down from the ground multiple times, and this can provide a full-body workout. The movement of the arms and legs can also provide exercise benefits.

Balance: Drawing Kolam requires standing on one foot or shifting weight from one foot to another while creating the patterns. This can help improve balance and stability.

Core strength: Drawing Kolam involves using the core muscles to maintain balance and support the body while creating the patterns. This can help improve core strength and stability.

Improves posture: Drawing Kolam involves maintaining a straight posture while squatting or bending. This can help improve posture and reduce the risk of back pain.

Calorie burning: Drawing Kolam is a physical activity that can burn calories. The amount of calories burned may vary depending on the intensity and duration of the activity.

Chapter 11: Kolam and Technology

Role of Technology in Kolam Making

Technology has now made it possible to create digital Kolams using various software applications. Here are some ways in which technology has impacted the art of Kolam making:

Digital Kolam designs: With the use of digital technology, it is now possible to create Kolam designs on a computer or mobile device. There are many software applications available that allow users to create intricate Kolam designs and patterns.

Mobile apps: There are now mobile apps that allow users to create digital Kolams using their phones or tablets. These apps offer a range of designs, colors, and patterns that can be customized to one's liking. This allows people to practice Kolam making anytime, anywhere, without the need for physical materials.

Augmented Reality: Augmented reality technology can be used to project digital kolam designs onto the ground, allowing people to create kolams without using traditional materials. This technology can also allow people to see how a design will look before they start drawing it on the ground.

Social media: People can now share their designs on social media platforms such as Instagram, Facebook, and Twitter, and receive feedback and appreciation from people all over the world. It is easier for people to share their Kolam designs with a wider audience. Social media has also played a role in preserving and promoting the traditional art form.

Online tutorials: With the help of technology, people can now access online tutorials that teach them how to create different types of Kolam designs. These tutorials are available in various formats, such as text, images, and videos, and can be accessed from anywhere in the world.

Digital preservation: With the use of digital technology, it is now possible to store and preserve traditional Kolam designs for future generations in Digital archives, ensuring they are not lost to time.

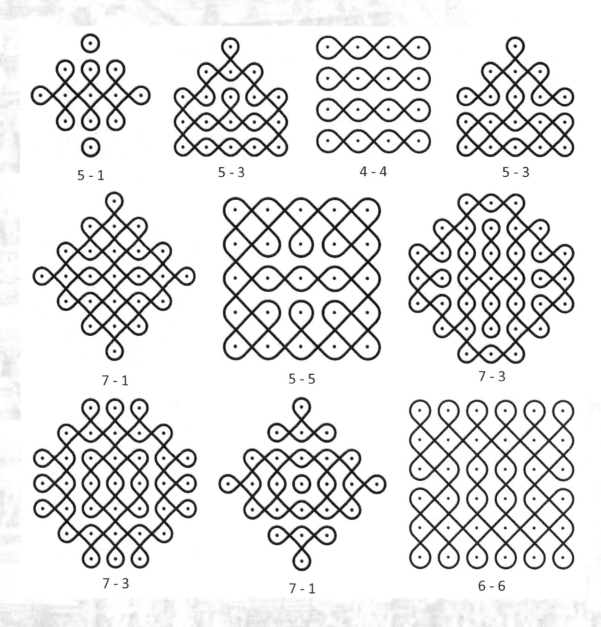

5 - 1   5 - 3   4 - 4   5 - 3

7 - 1   5 - 5   7 - 3

7 - 3   7 - 1   6 - 6

Projectors: Some people now use projectors to create large-scale Kolams on walls or floors. This allows for intricate designs to be created quickly and efficiently, without the need for physical materials.

3D printing: There are now 3D printers that can create physical Kolams using a range of materials such as plastic, wood, or metal. This allows for more intricate designs to be created with precision and accuracy.

Kolam in Digital Media and Social Networking Sites

Kolam, has gained popularity on digital media and social networking sites in recent years. Digital media and social networking sites provide a platform for artists to showcase their work, connect with other artists, and promote the art form to a global audience. Here are some ways in which Kolam has made its way and featured on digital media and social networking sites:

Instagram: Instagram has become a popular platform for sharing Kolam designs. Artists can use the platform to showcase their work, connect with other artists, and share their creative process. Several Instagram accounts dedicated to Kolam have gained a large following, providing a platform for artists to reach a wider audience.

3 - 3   5 - 3   4 - 4   5 - 3

7 - 1   5 - 5   7 - 3

7 - 3   7 - 1   6 - 6

YouTube: YouTube has become a popular platform for sharing tutorials and videos related to Kolam. There are several channels dedicated to Kolam, providing step-by-step instructions on how to create different designs. These channels have gained a large following, providing an opportunity for artists to share their knowledge and promote the art form.

Facebook: Facebook has several groups and pages dedicated to Kolam. These groups provide a platform for artists to connect with each other, share their work, and promote the art form. Facebook has also become a platform for organizing Kolam competitions and events.

Online communities: There are several online communities dedicated to Kolam, providing a platform for artists to connect and share their work. These communities provide an opportunity for artists to receive feedback on their work and connect with others who share a passion for the art form.

Showcase of creativity: Social media has become a platform for showcasing creativity, and Kolam is no exception. Artists can now showcase their work on social media platforms, reaching a wider audience and receiving recognition for their creativity.

5 - 3	5 - 3	4 - 4	5 - 3
7 - 1	5 - 5	7 - 3	
7 - 3	7 - 1	6 - 6	

Preservation of the art form: Social media has played a role in preserving and promoting the art form of Kolam. Through the sharing of designs, tutorials, and information, social media has helped to spread awareness and knowledge about Kolam.

Engagement with viewers: Social media has allowed artists to engage with their viewers and receive feedback on their work. This has created a dialogue between the artist and the viewer, allowing for a deeper appreciation and understanding of the art form.

Inspiration for new designs: Social media platforms have become a source of inspiration for Kolam artists. Artists can find new designs and variations on traditional patterns, which they can incorporate into their own work.

Innovation: Social media has provided a platform for innovation and experimentation with Kolam designs. Artists can now create digital designs and use software to enhance their creations, leading to new and exciting possibilities for the art form.

Global exposure: Social media has provided a platform for Kolam to gain global exposure. Artists from different parts of the world can share their work and collaborate with others, creating a diverse community of Kolam artists.

| 3 - 3 | 5 - 3 | 4 - 4 | 5 - 3 |

| 7 - 1 | 5 - 5 | 7 - 3 |

| 7 - 1 | 7 - 1 | 6 - 6 |

Use of Kolam in Branding and Marketing

Kolam, has been increasingly used in branding and marketing campaigns in recent years. Its intricate designs and vibrant colors have made it an attractive option for companies looking to create a unique and eye-catching brand identity. Here are some ways in which Kolam has been used in branding and marketing:

Logos and branding: Kolam designs have been used to create logos and brand identities for companies. The intricate patterns and bright colors of Kolam make it a distinctive and memorable visual element that can help a brand stand out from the competition.

Packaging and product design: Kolam designs have been used in product packaging and design, particularly in the food and beverage industry. The use of Kolam designs on packaging can evoke a sense of tradition and authenticity, making it an attractive option for brands that want to emphasize their heritage or cultural roots.

5 - 1	5 - 3	4 - 4	5 - 3
7 - 1	5 - 5	7 - 3
7 - 3	7 - 1	6 - 6

Event decorations: Kolam designs have been used to decorate events, particularly in the hospitality industry. Kolam designs have been used to create visually stunning backdrops and installations at events such as product launches, exhibitions, conferences, weddings, and festivals. The intricate designs and vibrant colors of Kolam add a unique touch to event decor, creating a visually appealing and culturally rich atmosphere.

Social media marketing: Kolam designs have been used in social media marketing campaigns, particularly on platforms such as Instagram and Pinterest. Brands can use Kolam designs to create visually appealing posts that attract followers and promote their products or services.

Cultural associations: Companies that use Kolam designs in their branding and marketing campaigns can tap into the rich cultural associations of the art form. Kolam is often associated with ideas such as tradition, creativity, and mindfulness, and companies can use these associations to create a positive image for their brand.

Chapter 12: Evolution of Kolam

Evolution and Adaptation of Kolam

Kolam has evolved and adapted over time to reflect changing social, cultural, and technological influences. Here are some of the ways in which Kolam has evolved and adapted over time:

Materials and tools: The traditional materials used to create Kolam were rice flour and natural pigments. Today, artists use a wide range of materials and tools, including colored powders, paint, flowers, and even digital tools such as software and apps. This has allowed for greater experimentation and creativity in the art form.

Designs and styles: Kolam designs have evolved over time, reflecting changes in society and culture. While traditional designs often feature geometric patterns and floral motifs, artists now create designs based on a wide range of themes, from nature and spirituality to pop culture and movie characters to social issues.

Globalization: The globalization of culture has had an impact on Kolam, with artists incorporating elements from other cultures into their designs. For example, some Kolam artists now incorporate elements of Western art styles and designs in their work. This has created a hybrid form of Kolam that reflects the diversity and complexity of the modern world.

Technological innovation: Kolam has adapted to technological innovations, with artists using digital tools and platforms to create and share their designs. This has led to new and exciting possibilities for the art form, including the creation of 3D and animated Kolam designs.

Location: While Kolam was traditionally made on the floor outside homes, it is now created in a variety of locations, including on walls, on paper, and even on digital platforms. This has allowed the art form to reach a wider audience and adapt to new contexts.

Meaning: The meaning of Kolam has also evolved over time. While it was originally seen as a way of bringing good luck and warding off evil, it is now also seen as a way of expressing creativity, mindfulness, and community.

Sustainability: With growing awareness of environmental issues, Kolam has adapted to incorporate eco-friendly materials and practices. For example, artists now use natural materials and dyes in their work, and some Kolams are made using rice flour or other biodegradable substances.

Learning and Preserving the Art of Kolam

Learning and preserving the art of Kolam is essential for keeping this rich cultural tradition alive. Here are some ways in which the art of Kolam can be learned and preserved:

Traditional teaching methods: Kolam has traditionally been learned through observation, practice, and repetition, with younger generations learning from their elders. This traditional method of teaching is still widely used today, with families and communities passing down the art form to their children and grandchildren.

Formal education: One way to preserve the art of Kolam is through formal education. This includes incorporating Kolam into school curriculums and offering courses and workshops. This ensures that future generations have the skills and knowledge to carry on this tradition.

5 - 1   5 - 3   4 - 4   5 - 3

7 - 1   5 - 5   7 - 3

7 - 3   7 - 1   6 - 6

Documenting and archiving: Documenting and archiving the art of Kolam is crucial for preserving this cultural tradition. This can include collecting and cataloging traditional designs, documenting the process of creating Kolam, and recording the stories and histories associated with the art form. This can help to ensure that the art form is accessible to future generations.

Advocacy and support: Advocacy and support from government, NGOs, and private organizations are crucial to preserving the art of Kolam. This includes providing funding and resources for preservation efforts, promoting the art form to wider audiences, and advocating for the recognition and protection of Kolam as a cultural heritage.

Workshops and classes: Kolam workshops and classes can be organized to teach people the techniques and skills needed to create Kolam. These can be conducted by experienced artists, cultural organizations, or educational institutions.

Cultural exchange: Cultural exchange programs can help to preserve the art of Kolam by facilitating exchanges between practitioners and enthusiasts from different regions and cultures. This can lead to the development of new techniques and styles, as well as greater appreciation and understanding of the tradition.

Online resources: The internet offers a wealth of resources for learning and preserving the art of Kolam. There are many websites, videos, and blogs that offer tutorials, tips, and inspiration for creating Kolam. Social media platforms such as Instagram, YouTube and Facebook also offer a platform for artists to share their work and connect with others.

Community engagement: Kolam is a communal art form, and engaging with communities is crucial to preserving it. This includes organizing Kolam competitions, exhibitions, and festivals, as well as inviting experts to speak and teach about the art form. This can help to create a sense of pride and appreciation for the tradition.

The Impact of Modernization on Kolam

The impact of modernization on Kolam, a traditional art form from South India, has been both positive and negative. Here are some of the ways in which modernization has impacted Kolam:

| 5 - 3 | 5 - 3 | 4 - 4 | 5 - 3 |

| 7 - 1 | 5 - 5 | 7 - 3 |

| 7 - 3 | 7 - 1 | 6 - 6 |

Change in materials: One of the most significant impacts of modernization on Kolam is the use of modern materials such as synthetic colors and chalk powder instead of traditional materials like rice flour and natural pigments. While this has made the art form more accessible and convenient, it has also led to a loss of traditional techniques and skills.

Changes in designs and styles: Modernization has brought about changes in the designs and styles of Kolam. Traditional designs have been replaced with more modern, geometric patterns, and new designs have been created that incorporate elements of popular culture, such as movie characters and logos.

Changes in purpose and context: With the rise of modernization, the purpose and context of Kolam have also changed. While Kolam was traditionally created as a daily ritual to honor the goddess of wealth and prosperity, today it is often created for decorative purposes and as a form of self-expression.

Decline in traditional knowledge: The loss of daily ritual and traditional techniques has also led to a decline in the transmission of traditional knowledge about Kolam. Younger generations may not

have the same exposure to Kolam as previous generations, and there is a risk that traditional knowledge may be lost over time.

Impact on social norms: Modernization has also led to changes in social norms that can impact the creation and appreciation of Kolam. For example, the rise of high-rise buildings and urbanization has led to a loss of space and time for creating Kolam. This can impact the practice and appreciation of the art form.

Increased visibility and global reach: Modernization has also increased the visibility of Kolam. With the rise of social media and digital platforms, Kolam designs are now being shared and appreciated by a wider audience, both within India and across the world. Modernization has also led to an increased global reach for Kolam, with artists and enthusiasts from around the world discovering and practicing the art form.

Commercialization: Modernization has also led to the commercialization of Kolam. The art form is now used in branding and marketing, and artists may create designs for commercial purposes rather than as a form of self-expression. This can lead to a loss of authenticity and cultural significance.

Future of Kolam

The future of Kolam, a traditional art form from South India, is both promising and uncertain. Here are some of the ways in which the future of Kolam may unfold:

Embracing technology: The use of technology in creating Kolam is likely to increase in the future. Already, artists are using digital tools to create Kolam designs, and this trend is likely to continue. This can lead to new and exciting designs and techniques but also raises questions about the authenticity of the art form.

Adapting to changing times: As social norms continue to change, the practice of creating Kolam may need to adapt to fit into modern lifestyles. This could mean creating smaller designs or using varied materials and techniques that are more suited to urban living.

Sustainable practices: In order for Kolam to have a future, it is important to consider sustainable practices. This includes using eco-friendly materials, promoting responsible and ethical sourcing, and minimizing waste.

4 - 4   5 - 3   4 - 4   5 - 3

7 - 1   5 - 5   7 - 3

7 - 3   7 - 1   6 - 6

Innovation and creativity: Kolam have always been an art form that evolves and adapts over time. In the future, artists may continue to innovate and experiment with new materials, techniques, and designs. This could lead to the creation of new and exciting styles of Kolam that reflect the changing times.

Recognition and appreciation: The future of Kolam also depends on recognition and appreciation from wider audiences. As Kolam gains more visibility and exposure, it may become a more widely recognized and appreciated art form, both within India and globally.

Preservation and education: Finally, education and preservation efforts are crucial to ensuring that the art of Kolam continues to thrive in the future. This includes documenting and archiving traditional designs and techniques, offering courses and workshops on the art form, and engaging with communities to promote appreciation and understanding of the tradition.

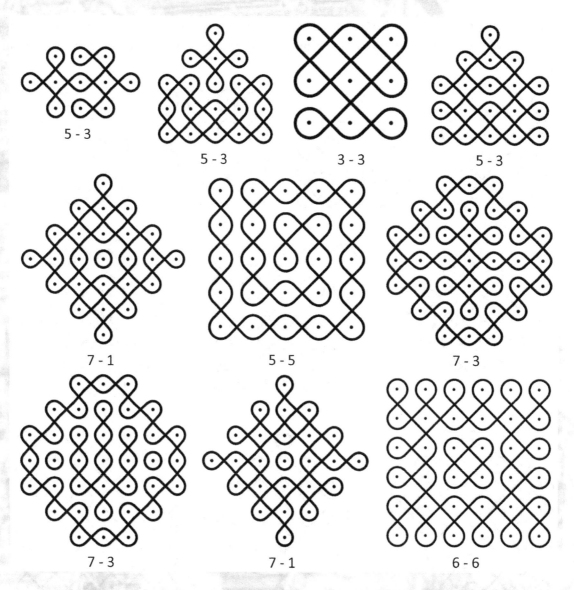

Made in the USA
Monee, IL
17 November 2024

70359375R10077